"Fascinating . . . You are not merely _____ a book; you are holding a key to the doors of perception. *Legally Stoned* is far more than an excellent, meticulously researched sourcebook; it is a highly readable treasure trove of experiments and experiences."

—Kinky Friedman, musician novelist, and politician

"*Legally Stoned* is a well-researched sourcebook for anyone interested in psychoactive substances that are currently legal in the United States. *Legally Stoned* cites scientific research and personal accounts to provide accurate descriptions of each substance's history, physiological effects, and the risks of use. *Legally Stoned* also challenges the rationality of the drug laws by describing the methods people often use to obtain and prepare each substance."

—Krystle Cole, www.NeuroSoup.com, author of *Lysergic* and *After the Trip*

"I refuse to plunge into paranoid speculation of why many of the magical and sacred foods of the gods are made illegal and their communicants vilified. Instead, I bless and give thanks for books such as this, and intelligent and courageous souls such as Dr. Thies for their efforts to keep the doors of perception in full view for all of us to see."

—Lon Milo DuQuette, author of *My Life with the Spirits* and *Enochian Vision Magick*

"Todd Thies is the new millennium's Timothy Leary. His book covers the unexplored, mind-blowing universe outside of the DEA's crosshairs with insight and clarity. *Legally Stoned* is a fascinating read, a guided journey down the rabbit hole."

—M. Chris Fabricant, author of *Busted! Drug War Survival Skills*

LEGALLY

stoned

14 Mind-Altering Substances You Can Obtain and Use Without Breaking the Law

TODD THIES, PH.D.

Citadel Press
Kensington Publishing Corp.
www.kensingtonbooks.com

CITADEL PRESS BOOKS are published by

Kensington Publishing Corp.
850 Third Avenue
New York, NY 10022

Printed in the United States of America

ISBN-13: 978-0-8065-3111-3

To my wife.

Contents

Foreword
by Kinky Friedman

You are not merely holding a book; you are holding a key to the doors of perception. Were you to experiment with some of the fourteen mind-altering substances in *Legally Stoned*, you might not break the law but you'd probably get high enough to go duck hunting with a rake. I've tried four of Dr. Thies's concoctions myself and I got so high I needed a stepladder to scratch my ass. (Haven't tried toad venom yet. I'm saving that one for Purim or the next time I'm on Bill O'Reilly, whichever comes first.)

Heracleitus once said that a man never steps in the same river twice. That is because the river changes and the man changes. Dr. Thies makes it clear that for thousands of years man has been changing, chemically, spiritually, politically. Thoreau's "quiet desperation," though, appears to be built into the human race.

Another way of belaboring this theme is to quote my personal guru, the Hillbilly Dalai Lama, Willie Nelson, who, while smoking a joint the size of a large kosher salami, once told me, "If you ain't crazy, there's something wrong with you."

Seen in the pale light of the twenty-first century, according to Dr. Thies, the war on drugs currently being waged by our government at the DEA is not only futile and counterproductive, but it runs inexplicably, inexorably against the grain of the Declaration of Independence. We tried prohibition once, Dr. Thies points out, and it created many more problems than it resolved.

Dr. Thies recommends, of course, that before you partake of "The CIA's Magic Beans" (*Andadenanthera peregrina*/colubrina seeds) or the "Gift from the Green Fairy" *(Artemisia absinthium)*—or anything else in this book—you should consult your lawyer and your doctor. I understand why the good professor might have included this disclaimer, but I think it's a waste of time to see a lawyer. As I always say, "Where there's a will, there's a lawyer." As far as doctors go, I vividly recall the last time I went to one.

"I've got some bad news for you," he told me. "You're going to have to quit masturbating."

"Why?" I shouted.

"Because I have to examine you," he said.

All this notwithstanding, *Legally Stoned* is far more than an excellent, meticulously researched sourcebook; it is a highly readable treasure trove of experiments and experiences—empirical, existential, eternal as the human spirit—guaranteed to goose you, at least for the moment, out of that monotonous mortal groove. For what is life if not moments, all strung together like a necklace made of morning glory and Hawaiian baby woodrose seeds?

So should you consult your doctor or lawyer before at-
tempting to replicate some of these experiments outside the
lab? I believe there are other voices you should listen to. One
of them is the still, small voice within. If you look around at a
world full of slums and suburbs and Starbucks, perhaps you'll
hear that voice in three-part harmony with Alice in Wonderland and Jim Morrison. Then, of course, there's always the
voice of Bob Dylan, who once suggested everybody must get
stoned.

Dr. Thies, I believe, is an exemplary Virgil; he has performed the high spiritual task of the Wal-Mart greeter, asking
each one of us, "How can I help you?" If you read this new,
and certain to be controversial, book, I guarantee you'll find
it fascinating. If you decide to put the ancient key in the door,
God knows what might happen.

As my personal guru Uncle Willie often says, "Fortunately,
we're not in control."

As I often say, "Why the hell not?"

Medina, Texas
August 11, 2008

Acknowledgments

I have been gathering the information and experiences related in this book for more than twenty years. Without the previous work of certain individuals who are pioneers in the fields of psychoactive substances and entheogens, this book would have been very difficult, if not impossible, to write. First among these individuals are Fire and Earth Erowid, who run an Internet site containing a wealth of information on psychoactive substances. Their website was founded in 1995 with the initial focus being on entheogens. Over the years it has expanded to provide information on all mind-altering substances, becoming the online encyclopedia of psychoactive substances. The website is located at www.erowid.org.

The work of Jonathon Ott has also been of significant help in writing this book, especially his book *Pharmacotheon: Entheogenic Drugs, Their Plant Sources, and History.* Two other pioneers that deserve mention are Alexander and Ann Shulgin, and their books *Pihkal: A Chemical Love Story,* and *Tih-kal: The Continuation.*

I must thank my wife, who has been both my support and proofreader. I want to also thank my family, especially my parents and my sister and her family. Lastly, I want to thank all those that have contributed experiences with the various substances described in the book. Many of my friends have been willing, and sometimes regretful, experimenters with me. I have chosen to leave the identities of these experimenters anonymous in order to protect them from unwanted scrutiny.

LEGALLY
Stoned

INTRODUCTION

The "Drug War" may have begun in the twentieth century, but drug use seems to have been a part of human activity for thousands of years. While conducting research for this book, I was struck repeatedly by the observation that the use of mind-altering substances occurred in most (possibly all) cultures in the world. Most of the world's cultures also had a long history of psychoactive substance use, which often was an important part of the cultures' activities.

While in graduate school, I did research on people's use of psychoactive substances to alter mental and physical levels of arousal. The exact definition of arousal has received much debate and is the subject of a great volume of scientific research. Simply put, though, arousal is an individual's physiological and psychological state of excitement, energy, or activation. It is typically measured on at least one continuum, which can range from a low arousal state of deep sleep to a high arousal state of great excitement or terror. People can usually differentiate arousal states along this continuum. Most would agree that feeling relaxed is a lower arousal state than feeling worried, and that feeling angry is a higher arousal state than feeling calm. Levels of arousal can be obtained through physical tests (e.g., a polygraph, more commonly referred to as a lie detector test). Arousal levels can also be assessed by administering someone a psychological test.

By 1991, when I was doing my graduate research, it had been well established that people find certain arousal states more pleasant than others. Entire books have been written about which factors may determine what level of arousal an individual finds most pleasant at a given moment. One's desired arousal level differs among people, the time of day, the situation, and other factors.

Because humans have a desire to obtain certain arousal states, we use a variety of methods to reach them. My graduate research examined how people use psychoactive substances to alter their arousal states. Drug users who preferred substances that are a physiological stimulant (i.e., increase arousal) drugs, like methamphetamines or cocaine, also reported liking relatively high levels of arousal. Those who preferred relatively low levels of arousal liked substances that were physiological depressants (i.e., decreased arousal) such as heroin or valium.

Some substances did not fit this pattern. For example, those individuals who preferred alcohol to other substances were a mix of people seeking low arousal and those seeking high arousal, even though alcohol is a physiological depressant. It appears that some folks drink alcohol to "party" and increase their level of arousal. In addition to being a physiological depressant, alcohol also reduces inhibitions and makes it easier to engage in arousal-increasing behavior. Physiological and psychological measures of arousal indicate that some alcohol users have an increase in arousal following alcohol use. Other users imbibe alcohol for its physiological depressant effects in order to relax and decrease their arousal. Even those who drink alcohol to increase arousal will eventually have a decrease in arousal, as the depressant effects of the alcohol overpower any arousal-increasing effects created from "partying." Of course, getting a massage, reading a good book while sitting in front of a fireplace, riding on a roller coaster, and jumping out of airplanes are also all methods people use to alter their arousal use. Use of psychoactive substances is just an effective, rapid method that people have used for at least thousands of years.

Studies of nonhuman animals have found that many animals also engage in the use of intoxicating substances if they are able to. In a book titled *Intoxication: The Universal Drive for Mind-Altering Substances,* the author Ronald Siegel reviews the research on animal use of psychoactive substances. Dr. Siegel, who is a psychopharmacologist, presents a lengthy list of examples of humans and nonhuman animals using mind-altering substances.

Many animals, including species of monkeys, seek out and ingest partially fermented fruit and apparently get intoxicated by its alcohol content. Anyone who has observed the excited intoxication of a cat with catnip has seen an animal that seeks out a substance to seemingly get high.

A study by Shrai, Tsuda, Kitagawa, Naitoh, Seki, Kamimura, and Morohashi, published in the *Journal of American Mosquito Control Association* in June 2002, demonstrated that even some insects like their liquor. These researchers performed a study that examined whether a person's alcohol consumption affected his or her likelihood of being bitten by mosquitoes. The study showed that mosquitoes were more likely to bite an individual when he or she had been drinking alcohol than when the person was sober. There is more than one way to interpret the results of this study, but the results suggest that mosquitoes like to party.

Dr. Siegel's twenty-plus years of research and examination of the literature led him to conclude that the use of mind-altering substances was so pervasive among humans of all times and cultures, that the desire for such substances was a "fourth drive." By fourth drive, he was concluding that the drive to use mind-altering substances was equivalent to the three commonly recognized drives for food, water, and sex.

All human beings are born with the innate capacity to get high from a number of natural and manmade substances. Our brains are filled with neurons (nerve cells) that automatically respond to certain substances by changing a person's mental experience.

Heroin acts on our brain's nerve cells just like our own internal endorphins. It is because the human brain already has an existing mechanism to produce pleasure in place that the heroin molecule is able to tap into that same brain mechanism and produce its effects. If our brains had not developed to be reactive to psychoactive substances and if the brain did not already have a mechanism to respond to these substances, then there would be no such thing as psychoactive drug use.

Humans have developed in such a way that they want to alter their consciousness; therefore, it is only natural that people will seek out psychoactive substances.

The United States Declaration of Independence states: "We hold these truths to be self-evident, that all men are created equal, that they are endowed by their Creator with certain unalienable Rights, that among these are Life, Liberty and the pursuit of Happiness." In other words, there are certain rights that all people have and that no government has the power to take away.

The Declaration of Independence further states that "to secure these rights, Governments are instituted among Men, deriving their just powers from the consent of the governed,— That whenever any Form of Government becomes destructive of these ends, it is the Right of the People to alter or to abolish it, and to institute new Government, laying its foundation on such principles and organizing its powers in such form, as to them shall seem most likely to effect their Safety and Happiness." Thus, all of government's power comes from the people it governs.

Government does not make decisions independent of its people, and those in government cannot make choices that go against the will of the governed. Furthermore, because the government is one of the people, and because government's responsibility is to protect the "unalienable Rights" of its people, the people are right in altering or even abolishing the government.

What right can be more basic and unalienable than the right to choose what I put into my own body? I consider that eating broccoli, potato chips, or hash brownies are all things that are basic, unalienable rights. I also believe that a lot of people agree with me. This makes it our right to eat these things and to "alter" our government to allow us to do so.

The United States government made one attempt to go against the will of many of the governed when it instituted the prohibition of alcohol in 1920. This made the sale, transportation, and manufacture of alcohol illegal. Strangely, the amendment did not state that the use of alcohol was illegal.

Thirteen years later, prohibition of alcohol would be repealed with the 21st Amendment to the United States Constitution. The major argument for re-legalizing alcohol was that the problems created from prohibition were greater than the problems caused by allowing people to use alcohol legally. Also, many people continued to use alcohol under prohibitions, so it was not as though the problems of alcohol went away.

A range of social problems were a direct result of prohibition. A violent black market for alcohol developed. Stronger liquors became more popular because their potency made them more profitable. Tax revenues from alcohol were replaced by an enforcement cost of many hundreds of millions of dollars. With the repeal of prohibition in 1933, the black market for alcohol mostly disappeared. The organized crime that developed during prohibition did not go away, but ventured into other illegal activities, such as dealing narcotics. In addition to the woes created by prohibition, it is this writer's belief that many politicians supported the repeal of prohibition because they really wanted to have a drink.

Despite the country's recognition of the problems that alcohol prohibition caused, our leaders have created prohibition of many other psychoactive substances that Americans wish to use. Many of these substances are arguably less harmful than the legal drugs alcohol and tobacco.

The Controlled Substances Act is the United States' current attempt at drug prohibition. It was passed as part of the Comprehensive Drug Abuse Prevention and Control Act of 1970. It eventually gave the Drug Enforcement Agency (DEA), founded in 1973, the power to control drugs without having to go through Congress for approval to make rulings regarding substances it wants to regulate.

The Congress does have the power to go against DEA decisions, and it appears to have done so at one point when the DEA wanted to further restrict the availability of pseudoephedrine.

The Act set up five schedules that classify drugs at the DEA's discretion. Schedule I drugs have a high potential for abuse, they have no currently accepted medical use (according to the DEA's judgment), and there is a lack of accepted safety for use of the drug. Schedule II drugs have a high potential for abuse and dependence, but unlike Schedule I drugs, they do have a currently accepted medical use. Schedule III drugs have some potential for abuse, but less than those in Schedules I and II. These drugs also have some currently accepted medical use. Schedule IV drugs have a low potential for abuse relative to Schedule III and above drugs, and the drugs have a currently accepted medical use. They also have limited risk of dependence. Schedule V drugs have the lowest potential risk of abuse or dependency, and they have a currently accepted medical use.

The drugs that the United States government has decided that you have no right to use no matter what (i.e., Schedule I), are as follows:

Chemical Name	Common Name
1-(1-phenylcyclohexyl)pyrrolidine	[PCPy, PHP, rolicyclidine]
1-(2-phenylethyl)-4-phenyl-4-acetoxypiperidine	[PEPAP, synthetic heroin]
1-1-(2-thienyl)cyclohexyl piperidine	[TCP, tenocyclidine]
1-1-(2-thienyl)cyclohexyl pyrrolidine	[TCPy]
1-methyl-4-phenyl-4-propionoxypiperidine	[MPPP, synthetic heroin]
2,5-dimethoxy-4-ethylamphetamine	[DOET]
2,5-dimethoxyamphetamine	[DMA, 2,5-DMA]
3,4,5-trimethoxyamphetamine	[TMA]
3,4-methylenedioxyamphetamine	[MDA, Love Drug]
3,4-methylenedioxyamethamphetamine	[MDMA, Ecstasy, XTC]
3,4-methylenedioxy-N-ethylamphetamine	[N-ethyl MDA, MDE, MDEA]
3-methylfentanyl	[China White, fentanyl]
3-methylthiofentanyl	[China White, fentanyl]
4-bromo-2,5-dimethoxyamphetamine	[DOB, 4-bromo-DMA]
4-bromo-2,5-dimethoxyphenethylamine	[Nexus, 2-CB]
4-methoxyamphetamine	[PMA]
4-methyl-2,5-dimethoxyamphetamine	[DOM, STP]
4-methylaminorex	[U4Euh, McN-422]
5-methoxy-3,4-methylenedioxy amphetamine	[MMDA]
acetorphine	
acetyl-alpha-methylfentanyl	
acetyldihydrocodeine	[acetylcodone]
acetylmethadol	[methadyl acetate]
allylprodine	
alphacetylmethadol except levo-alphacetylmethadol	
alpha-ethyltryptamine	[ET, Trip]

Chemical Name	Common Name
alphameprodine	
alphamethadol	
alpha-methylfentanyl	[China White, fentanyl]
alpha-methylthiofentanyl	[China White, fentanyl]
aminorex	
benzethidine	
benzylmorphine	
betacetylmethadol	
beta-hydroxy-3-methylfentanyl	[China White, fentanyl]
beta-hydroxyfentanyl	[China White, fentanyl]
betameprodine	
betamethadol	
betaprodine	
bufotenine	[mappine, N,N-dimethylserotonin]
cathinone	
codeine methylbromide	
codeine-N-oxide	
cyprenorphine	
desomorphine	
dextromoramide	[Palfium, Jetrium, Narcolo]
diampromide	
diethylthiambutene	
diethyltryptamine	[DET]
difenoxin	[Lyspafen]
dihydromorphine	
dimenoxadol	
dimepheptanol	
dimethylthiambutene	
dimethyltryptamine	[DMT]

Chemical Name	Common Name
dioxaphetyl butyrate	[Dipipan, phenylpiperone HC1, Diconal, Wellconal]
dipipanone	
drotebanol	[Metebanyl, oxymethebanol]
ethylmethylthiambutene	
etonitazene	
etorphine (except HC1)	
etoxeridine	
fenethylline	[Captagon, amfetyline, ethyltheophylline amphetamine]
furethidine	
gama hydroxybutyric acid	[GHB, gama hydroxybutyrate, sodium oxybate]
heroin	[diacetylmorphine, diamorphine]
hydromorphinol	
hydroxypethidine	
ibogaine	
ketobemidone	[Cliradon]
levomoramide	
levophenacylmorphan	
lysergic acid diethylamide	[LSD, lysergide, acid]
marijuana	[Cannabis]
mecloqualone	[Nubarene]
mescaline	
methaqualone	[Quaalude, Parest, Somnafac, Opitimil, Mandrax]
methcathinone	[N-methylcathinone, cat]
methyldesorphine	

Chemical Name	Common Name
methyldihydromorphine	
morpheridine	
morphine methylbromide	
morphine methylsulfonate	
morphine-N-oxide	
myrophine	
N,N-dimethylamphetamine	
N-ethyl-1-phenylcyclohexylamine	[PCE]
N-ethyl-3-piperidyl benzilate	[JB 323]
N-ethylamphetamine	[NEA]
N-hydroxy-3,4-methylenedioxy amphetamine	[N-hydroxy MDA]
nicocodeine	
nicomorphine	[Vilan]
N-methyl-3-piperidyl benzilate	[JB 336]
noracymethadol	
norlevorphanol	
normethadone	[Phenyldimazone]
normorphine	
norpipanone	
para-fluorofentanyl	[China White, fentanyl]
parahexyl	[Synhexyl]
peyote	
phenadoxone	
phenampromide	
phenomorphan	
phenoperidine	[Operidine, Lealgin]
pholcodine	[Copholco, Adaphol, Codisol, Lantuss, Pholcolin]

Chemical Name	Common Name
piritramide	[Piridolan]
proheptazine	
properidine	
propiram	[Algeril]
psilocin	
psilocybin	
racemoramide	
tetrahydrocannabinols	[THC, Delta-8 THC, Delta-9 THC],
thebacon	[Acetylhydrocodone, Acedicon, Thebacetyl]
thiofentanyl	[Chine white, fentanyl]
tilidine	[Tilidate, Valoron, Kitadol, Lak, Tilsa]
trimeperidine	[Promedolum]

The above are only those substances listed under Schedule I by the DEA. These substances have been made illegal without the consent of those governed. Not only are they placed there without the consent of the governed, they can be placed there in direct opposition to the will of the governed.

The issue of the medical use of marijuana demonstrates the United States government's refusal (and specifically that of DEA officials) to follow the principles set forth in the Declaration of Independence. This founding document of the United States asserts that "Governments are instituted among Men, deriving their just powers from the consent of the governed." The State of California has passed a law that marijuana should be available to those that have a doctor's prescription or letter to treat their illness. A large body of data indicates that marijuana is an effective treatment for certain medical problems. Despite this, the official stance of the DEA continues to be that marijuana has no currently accepted medical use. While the people governed have clearly indicated by their vote that they want marijuana to be provided to people for medical purposes, the federal government, via the DEA, continues to consider those who use marijuana for medical purposes to be criminals.

It is human nature to want to alter one's consciousness. All humans try to alter their consciousness. Not all of us use a substance to accomplish this, but a large portion of the human race does. The failure of alcohol prohibition did not demonstrate to those individuals in control of the DEA the futility of trying to prevent people from using substances to alter their consciousness. The basic urge to alter one's consciousness makes the current drug war futile.

How to Read This Book

Each substance described in the book has its own chapter. Each chapter is divided into five sections:

1. Description and History
2. Chemistry and Physiological Effects
3. How People Obtain and Use (the Substance)
4. The (Substance) Experience
5. Some Risks of Using (the Substance)

Section 1, "Description and History," provides the earliest documented descriptions of the use of the substance. The substance's social and cultural relevance is discussed where possible. This section of each chapter was the most interesting to research and write. I was repeatedly amazed by the significant role many of these psychoactive substances played in people's lives and by the important role they played in human history.

I also provide information about the legal status of each substance described. Though all of the substances described have been legally obtained by people, the exact legal status of the different substances varies. The legal status of the substances described can fit roughly into three categories.

1. *Substances that are completely legal in most, if not all, parts of the United States.* These substances are *Amanita muscaria* mushrooms, betel nuts, kava-kava, kratom, morning glory seeds, nutmeg, and *Salvia divinorum.*

2. *Substances that are legal to buy, but their purchase or use is regulated in some way.* Examples of these substances are *Artemesia absinthium,* dextromethorphan, and nitrous oxide.

3. *Substances that can be legally obtained but that contain an illegal substance.* These substances are *Anadenathera* seeds (containing bufotenine and DMT), *Bufo alavarius* toad venom (containing bufotenine), ayahuasca (containing DMT), and San Pedro cactus (containing mescaline). Law enforcement has typically not interfered with people buying or selling these (and they are easily available online), but there are occasional exceptions. Despite law enforcement's historical hands-off approach, there

is always the possibility that one could be arrested for buying or selling this third group of natural substances.

The "Chemistry and Physiological Effects" section of each chapter provides information regarding the chemicals involved in producing psychoactive effects and how the substance affects the body. The amount of information available on any given substance varied greatly, so some of these substances have been researched at great length, while others have been researched minimally. This section is meant to provide some general information to the reader and to be a starting point for the reader's own study.

The section "How People Obtain and Use [the Substance]" provides detailed information of how others have gotten the substance and used it for its psychoactive effects. I am not recommending that anyone follow the methods I have described. I provide this detailed information because I think it is important to show exactly how people are getting around our government's oppression in order to illuminate my point about the futility of the Drug War.

For every substance there is general information on how to find sources for purchasing the product. There are also specific sources that sell the substances provided for most items. All of these sources are recommended based upon the author's experience or the positive experiences of others, but this is no guarantee of continued good service or products.

In addition to these sites, it is also recommended that readers consider the source affiliated with the author, located at www.giftsfromtheancients.com. Gifts from the Ancients provides only top-quality legal psychoactives. The author can personally guarantee only the substances sold there, but readers are encouraged to try any of the recommended sites.

In this section of the book, information is also provided about the dosages typically used and the effects of these dosages. The amount of a dosage that is psychoactive and the effects of a particular dose of a substance will always be highly variable. Many factors, including a person's weight, how much food one has eaten, individual sensitivities, potencies of the substance, past experiences with psychoactive substances, psychological problems, and other variables can drastically alter how one is affected by a substance.

On the subject of dosage, an interesting article by Jose Stevens, Ph.D., published in the *Multidisciplinary Association for Psychedelic Studies (MAPS) Bulletin,* Volume 4, Number 4, described a dangerous usage pattern he called "macho ingestion syndrome." The name may seem somewhat comical, but the issue he is addressing is important. Dr. Stevens noted a trend in which some individuals felt that by ingesting very high dosages of a psychoactive/psychedelic substance, they somehow were superior or more "macho" than others who took a smaller dose. Stevens also noted that those who felt most "macho" by their high dose also felt that they were spiritually superior to other individuals. As a psychologist who has spent his career studying the use of psychoactive substances and those who use them, I have seen that such a perspective is most often the result of unhealthy personality. How one uses the psychedelic experience often determines one's mental health. Getting really wasted just for the purpose of getting really wasted is usually a sign of problems, not of some sort of superiority.

The section "The [Substance] Experience" provides descriptions of what people who use the substance have experienced. This includes both mental and physical effects. Individual reactions to a substance can vary greatly, and some individuals are particularly sensitive or resistant to specific substances.

The descriptions provided are usually based on the most commonly reported effects of the substance. When available, actual experiences are provided of the effects of the substance described by people who have tried it. I have tried to obtain firsthand accounts directly from the person who had the experience wherever possible. The identities of those providing firsthand accounts directly to this writer have been kept anonymous to protect the individuals reporting them.

Each chapter ends with "Some Risks of Using [the Substance]." As has been discussed previously, all substances have some risk of use. People who use these substances choose to take the risk that is involved in their use.

There is always the issue of addiction. Addiction is commonly divided into two types: physical and psychological. Physical addiction is characterized by the body developing withdrawal symptoms when use of the substance is stopped and by the body developing tolerance (i.e., needing more of the substance to produce the same effect).

Substances that have a high risk of physical dependence are identified in this section. Psychological dependence is the desire to continually use a substance despite significant negative effects. All mind-altering substances have the risk of psychological dependence. Because this risk is common to all substances, it will only be discussed in this section if there is something different about psychological dependence with regards to the substance.

The title of this section states "some risks," and it means exactly what it says. This section contains information regarding *only some* of the risks involved in using the substance. It is by no means meant to be a comprehensive list of risks of using the substance.

The focus of the section is on risks specific to the substance being discussed, and I have not included risks that are common to all psychoactive substance use. For example, while under the influence of a substance there is the risk that an individual will do something that is dangerous or that they later regret. These substances alter you, so they alter how you behave. There are also individuals who will have a specific sensitivity to a substance. This can happen with all kinds of substances people ingest. Many, if not most, of the substances described lack adequate research to provide anything close to a complete list of risks to using the substance. This section should be just the beginning of one's research into the risks of using these substances.

CHAPTER 1

THE DIVINE MUSHROOM:
Amanita muscaria
(Fly Agaric, Ibo Tengutake)

Description and History

The *Amanita muscaria* mushroom is native to North America and Europe, but it has been spread to many other parts of the world. The name "fly agaric" comes from its use in Europe as an insecticide. *Amanita muscaria* has probably been ingested for its psychoactive effects for thousands of years.

R. Gordon Wasson, in his book *Soma: Divine Mushroom of Immortality,* provides evidence that the mushroom is the "god-plant" the ancient Aryan (or Arya) civilization called Soma. The Aryan people were a migratory, cattle-herding people that moved from what is now Afghanistan to the Indian subcontinent about 3,500 years ago.

The Aryan people wrote a series of sacred hymns called Vedas that have become the foundation of the Hindu religion. The earliest of these Vedas (there are four Vedas in total) is the RigVeda, which speaks at length about Soma. Soma is described as having once been a god, but it is now a plant.

The plant is described as being red and juicy, and there is no mention of a stem or leaves. Ingesting the plant produces an ecstatic mental state. The Vedas indicate that the plant was found on mountainsides and gathered by moonlight. Liquid was squeezed from the plant and then mixed with milk. A portion of the Soma potion was dedicated to the gods, and the rest was drunk by those present.

In 1730, a Swedish man named Filip Johann von Strahlenberg, who had been a prisoner of war in Siberia for twelve years, described the use of *Amanita muscaria* mushrooms by the Siberian people. He reported that they would boil the mushrooms and then drink the liquid, "which intoxicates them." He also reported that those who could not afford the mushrooms would gather the urine of those who had drunk the liquid. They would then drink the urine "as having still some virtue of the mushroom in it, and by this way they also got drunk."

As bizarre as that sounds, in the later 1700s two members of a Russian expedition to the Kamchatka Peninsula, Stepan Krasheninnikov and Georg Wilhelm, published similar accounts of the mushroom liquid drinking and subsequent urine ingestion. A significant amount of the psychoactive chemicals of *Amanita muscaria* are secreted in the urine, making descriptions of people getting drunk from the urine plausible. Several other writers have since reported this urine-drug recycling by people in Siberia.

Several accounts of *Amanita muscaria* use by tribes living in Siberia and the Kamchatka Peninsula were published in the centuries following Strahlenberg's 1730 account. There were descriptions of use of the mushrooms for recreational as well as shamanic purposes.

When these areas became Communist under the Soviet Union in the early 1900s, reports of the use of *Amanita muscaria* ceased. This does not mean that use of the mushroom stopped, but that information about drug use was not viewed positively by the Soviet government. After the fall of communism in the area, the Estonian mycologist (i.e., someone who studies mushrooms) Maret Saar published information in 1991 that reported the continued use of *Amanita muscaria* mushrooms by people living on the Kamchatka Peninsula.

Amanita muscaria mushrooms also grow wild in North America. A statue of what appears to be an *Amanita muscaria* mushroom was found in Navarit, Mexico, dated to AD 100. This suggests that these mushrooms may have also been used by early North Americans.

In 1869, two German chemists, named Schmiedeberg and Koppe, published a book about an alkaloid they had isolated from *Amanita muscaria,* called muscarine. They falsely believed that muscarine was responsible for the mushroom's psychoactive properties. Though muscarine has some physical effects (e.g., increased sweating and salivation), it is not psychoactive. There is also very little muscarine present in *Amanita muscaria,* so its effects would be minimal.

There was also a report that bufotenine was present in *Amanita muscaria.* Bufotenine is a psychoactive chemical present in the venom of the *Bufo alavarius* toad. However, research has made it clear that *Amanita muscaria* does not contain bufotenine.

In 1964, the two chemicals responsible for the psychoactive effects of the mushroom were identified. These chemicals are ibotenic acid (alpha-amino-3-hydroxy-5-isoxazole acetic acid) and its decarboxylation byproduct muscimol (3-hydroxy-5-aminomethyl isoxazole). Muscimol is probably the cause of the psychoactive effects, and the body probably changes ibotenic acid into muscimol for it to be psychoactive. Ibotenic acid produces psychoactive effects in humans in dosages from 50 to 100 milligrams, and muscimol produces the same effect in dosages of 10 to 15 milligrams.

It typically takes two to three hours for the peak effects of *Amanita muscaria* to be felt, and the effects last for six to eight hours. After oral ingestion of ibotenic acid and/or muscimol a substantial amount of these are excreted in the urine. This lends credence to stories of Siberian people drinking the urine of those who have consumed the liquid obtained from *Amanita muscaria*.

Lewis Carrol, the author of *Alice in Wonderland*, was reportedly influenced by reports of the use of *Amanita muscaria*. There is a dispute about whether or not he actually used the mushroom, or if he had just read about it. Users of *Amanita muscaria* report many experiences that are similar to those reported in *Alice in Wonderland*.

In 1979, a religion dedicated to the mushroom was developed. The religion's founder is an individual named Hawk. Hawk was reportedly inspired by partaking of some *Amanita muscaria* tea on a "magical San Francisco evening." His experience led to an obsession with hunting down the mushrooms to make the "sacred soma," which would become the Eucharist of the new religion.

Fasting is a significant part of the religion's rituals, and Hawk reports that the *Amanita muscaria* mushrooms have appetite-suppressant properties to assist with this practice.

Hawk reported using a brew of the mushroom three times a day and ingesting it more than 10,000 times over a twenty-nine-year period.

His religion is apparently based upon a mixture of shamanism, ancient Indian Vedas that form part of the Hindu religion, and the Zend Avesta, which is a Zoroastrian text. His wife, Venus, began the regular use of the *Amanita muscaria* potion a couple of years after Hawk, and she has taken on the role of High Priestess. Hawk's website provides a wealth of information about his religion and the sacred mushroom. It is located at www.somashamans.com. A number of videos on which Hawk describes the mushroom and his religious belief can be found on Google by typing in "Hawk" and "amanita muscaria."

There is no federal law regulating *Amanita muscaria*. Thus it is legal to grow, buy, sell, and possess. If the mushrooms are sold as a supplement, then they must comply with federal laws regarding supplements. As a result, most companies that sell them label them as "not for human consumption."

A state law in Louisiana that went into effect in 2005 made it illegal in that state to consume *Amanita muscaria* mushrooms. The Louisiana law did not make it illegal to grow or possess the mushrooms for "aesthetic, landscaping, or decorative purposes." People in Louisiana still get their mushrooms; they just do not tell anyone they are going to eat them.

Chemistry and Physiological Effects

The molecular weight of muscimol is 114.10, and the molecular weight of ibotenic acid is 158.11. Muscimol's primary action is at gamma-aminobutyric-acid (GABA) sites in the brain. GABA is an inhibitory neurotransmitter. It is the most common inhibitory neurotransmitter found in vertebrate central nervous systems. By binding to sites in the brain, it causes the opening of ion channels to allow either the flow of negatively charged chloride ions into the cell or positively charged potassium out of the cell.

Muscimol also increases the presence of dopamine in many parts of the brain. This chemical has been shown to be active in several parts of the brain including the cerebral cortex, hippocampus, and cerebellum.

Ibotenic acid is partially metabolized into muscimol and the rest excreted. It is structurally similar to glutamate and activates NMDA receptors, but it probably needs to convert to muscimol to produce its psychoactive effects.

Commonly reported physical effects of *Amanita muscaria* are analgesia (decreased pain), physical relaxation, loss of equilibrium, pupil dilation resulting in blurred vision, increased salivation, increased perspiration, runny nose, watery eyes, muscle twitches, and nausea.

How People Obtain and Use *Amanita muscaria* Mushrooms

People obtain *Amanita muscaria* mushrooms for use in one of four ways:

1. Pick the mushrooms in the wild (a risky method)
2. Grow the mushrooms (a difficult, but possible method)
3. Purchase the dried mushrooms (a good method)
4. Buy *Amanita muscaria* extracts (the easiest and most intense method)

Picking the Mushrooms in the Wild

The *Amanita muscaria* mushroom has a large red top with white spots. It grows wild in most of the northern hemisphere and has spread to many parts of the southern hemisphere. It has a distinctive look and typically grows in large groups. Fully grown, the bright red cap is usually eight to twenty centimeters (three to eight inches) in diameter. The red color of the cap may fade in older mushrooms after a rain. The stem is white and grows five to twenty centimeters (two to eight inches) high.

The *Amanita muscaria* mushroom emerges from the soil looking like a white egg, covered in the white warty material of the universal veil. As the fungus grows, the red color appears through the broken veil and the cap changes from bell shaped to hemispherical, finally flattening when mature.

Amanita muscaria is most often found next to pine trees, but it is also commonly found with birch, spruce, and fir trees. Depending on the climate, it will fruit from summer through fall. The mushroom will typically appear in the same places each year, so one can return to the same spot every year to gather mushrooms.

Though the mushroom has a distinctive look, picking it in the wild is risky because its cousins are deadly poisonous. The two cousins that produce the most deaths are *Amanita phalloides* (death cap) and *Amanita virosa* (destroying angel). These two mushrooms are responsible for at least 90 percent of all poisonous mushroom deaths.

Luckily, though, these two mushrooms look different from *Amanita muscaria*. It is possible for someone who has taken the time to educate himself to fairly safely gather *Amanita muscaria* in the wild. In order to do so, one would need more information than is provided here. This education would include studying wild mushrooms to be very clear on the appearances of *Amanita* and other mushroom species.

The typical dosage of fresh *Amanita muscaria* is two to four mature caps.

Growing the Mushrooms

Attempts to grow the mushroom on lab mediums have been unsuccessful. The mushrooms have a symbiotic relationship with the pine, birch, spruce, or fir trees they grow near, and growing the mushroom must be done in nature.

Mushrooms are a type of fungi. Along with bacteria, the fungi play an important role in nature by breaking down plant and animal matter so that it can be utilized for the growth of future plants. These plants are in turn eaten by the animals to sustain their life. The plants and animals eventually die and the cycle starts all over again.

Amanita muscaria mushrooms belong to a category called mycorrhizal-symbiotic. This category of mushrooms lives at the base of a plant or tree and forms a symbiotic relationship. The mushroom gains certain chemicals or nutrients from the plant or tree, and in return the mushroom breaks down other nutrients and metals for use by its host.

In order to grow *Amanita muscaria,* it is best to obtain a spore print or spore syringe of the mushroom. A spore print is a piece of paper with mushroom spores on it. Spores are the way mushrooms reproduce. They are essentially mushroom seeds. A spore syringe is a syringe containing mushroom spores and water.

If one is lucky enough to have access to a live mushroom, it can be used for propagation. Dried mushrooms can also be used, but this method is the least reliable. One takes the spores or mushrooms and mixes them into the soil near the base of the appropriate tree (pines are best). The area should be watered at least every few days, unless rain does the job. Water is the most important thing for the growth of mushrooms. In their mature form, they are almost 90 percent water. They germinate best with a high rate of humidity.

Once established, the mushrooms should return each year. To obtain *Amanita muscaria* mushroom spore prints, type "amanita muscaria spore print" into any Internet search engine. A resource for *Amanita muscaria* spore prints is www. sporeworks.com. The website www.erowid.org/general/sub missions/links/links_reciprocal.shtml also contains many online resources for *Amanita muscaria* supplies.

The typical dosage for fresh *Amanita muscaria* is two to four caps.

Using Dried Amanita muscaria Mushrooms

In recent years (before the development of extracts), the most common method for using *Amanita* was to ingest dried *Amanita muscaria*. The typical oral dosage is 30 grams of dried caps. Obviously, the weight of the person will determine the dose needed.

The majority opinion is that dried mushrooms are less potent than fresh ones. Despite the possibility of decreased potency, dried *Amanita muscaria* mushrooms may have an advantage over the fresh product. Drying or heating the mushroom may convert some of the ibotenic acid into muscimol. This conversion is important because it appears that ibotenic acid is responsible for some of the negative effects of the mushrooms, such as the body's excessive sweating.

Doing a search on the Internet will provide many resources for dried *Amanita muscaria*. Here are some online resources:

www.giftsfromtheancients.com
www.iamshaman.com
www.bouncingbearbotanicals.com
www.ethnosupply.com

One can also smoke dried *Amanita muscaria*. Smoking typically leads to a quicker effect, but also a shorter effect. People who use this method crush the dried mushrooms into a pipe or bong.

Buying Amanita muscaria *Extract*

The most intense method of using *Amanita muscaria* is to buy an extract. This is a very new method. Resources for *Amanita muscaria* extracts include

www.ethnobotanicals.com
www.ethnosupply.com
www.psychoactiveherbs.com.

Of course, one can put "amanita muscaria extract" into most Internet search engines to get a list of many resources.

I have been unable to find dosage information from any of these sites. You may contact the site directly to ask for dosage information. They will be cautious about giving this information, because they cover themselves legally by saying that their products are not for human consumption. People who use extracts figure their dosages by comparing the typical (non-extract) dried mushroom dose to the similar extract dose. If the typical dosage of dried *Amanita muscaria* is 30 grams for an average weight adult, the dosage of 10× extract would be 3 grams. Similarly, the dosage of 25× extract would be 3/4th of a gram.

The *Amanita muscaria* Mushroom Experience

Oral ingestion of *Amanita muscaria* mushrooms produces effects within thirty minutes to one hour. The duration of the effects can vary from four to ten hours. Smoking the dried mushrooms will result in a more rapid onset of effects, but with a shorter duration. Smoking also seems to result in less intense effects.

Most people who use the mushrooms report experiencing nausea that often leads to vomiting. Nausea is much less common with smoking the mushroom. Some people feel that fasting before using the mushroom reduces this problem, but it may be that an empty stomach just means less to throw up. Typically having some food in the stomach reduces nausea when taking a substance that upsets the stomach, so people have to decide for themselves. The nausea usually subsides after a while, and by the time the psychoactive experience peaks, it is gone.

Emotionally, people often feel at peace and even euphoric. There is often marked analgesia (decreased pain response). The user usually feels relaxed, and at higher doses typically feels sedated and sleepy.

Daydreams, as well as actual dreams while asleep, are often described as particularly vivid. Feeling like one is lucid dreaming (i.e., awareness that one is dreaming) or having an out-of-body experience (i.e., astral projection) has often been reported. Hallucinations are sometimes reported, but they tend to be less intense than those experienced by users of many other hallucinogens, like LSD.

Synesthesia, where the senses get mixed together resulting in things like seeing sounds or tasting colors, is sometimes reported. Users tend to become more internally focused and the internal dialogue typically increases and intensifies. Socialization usually becomes more difficult and decreases.

Ataxia (impaired coordination) and loss of equilibrium are often reported. Increased salivation and sweating are common. In high doses, some people report feeling dissociated, as though they are not themselves, a sensation that can be unpleasant.

The majority of people report a mostly pleasant experience, but there is definitely the possibility of an unpleasant, anxiety-provoking experience, especially at higher doses.

College Sophomore Tries Amanitas

"I began by taking three caps that I had received from online a few days earlier. After about fifty minutes I think I was having a mild buzz, like after drinking a couple of beers. I decided to take one large cap that was in the bag. Trying to swallow this resulted in some serious need to vomit. A little came up, but with Pepto I was able to keep most of it down.

"I was listening to music and became more and more relaxed. It was pleasant except for the gnawing nausea. Due to being definitely sedated, I decided to sit up, turn off the music, and watch some TV. Lights took on a kind of halo effect, but I wouldn't call it exactly hallucinating. Things were more blurry than enhanced. Closing my eyes resulted in incredible visuals, but also contributed to my stomach upset, so I did not go with that.

"At some point I became pretty hot and sweaty and had to put a fan directly on me, which felt so good. The blowing air seemed intensified and I kick backed and enjoyed it. Time seemed kind of off and I think it did not last as long as it felt like it did. It was not exactly unpleasant, but I was ready to come down when I did. Oh, by the way, the whole stomach thing ended about the time I turned the fan on; it was certainly more pleasant after that point.

"I slept a lot afterward. I woke up a lot from pretty intense dreams, which I know was due to the mushrooms. There was probably some hangover given how much I slept, but by the time I got out of bed I felt fine, but really hungry."

Some Risks of Using *Amanita muscaria* Mushrooms

I have not been able to find any reports of addiction, dependency, or withdrawal from *Amanita muscaria*. There is one exception to this. Hawk, the founder of an *Amanita muscaria* religion, reported using the mushroom an average of three times a day for four and a half years. Despite the example of Hawk, *Amanita muscaria* has little risk of addiction, just like most psychedelics.

Typical side effects include nausea, drowsiness, loss of balance, sweating, and loss of coordination. The nausea is the most commonly reported negative effect of using these mushrooms.

I was unable to find any reports of injury due to *Amanita muscaria* intoxication, but the marked impairment in balance and coordination certainly puts a user at risk for physical injury if not careful. Obviously, a user should not drive under the influence; doing so would put himself or herself and others at risk.

A lot of disagreement remains about whether or not one can overdose on *Amanita muscaria*. In one report, someone took an extremely high dose of the mushroom and then had a heart attack. It is unknown, however, whether the mushroom was related to the heart attack.

A single case was reported anonymously in the Vernal Equinox, 1999 edition, of *The Entheogen Review,* which said that a person on a tricyclic antidepressant had convulsions after consuming *Amanita pantherina* mushrooms. The individual was taken to the hospital and had to be placed on artificial respiration for two hours. The person then awoke in apparently good health, with no memory for the negative experience.

Amanita pantherina are very similar to *Amanita muscaria*, and they contain the same psychoactive chemicals. Tricyclic antidepressants are an older class of medications for the treatment of depression. The more modern medications tend to have fewer side effects, with the same or greater effectiveness. Though these medications are less common these days, many people are still prescribed them, and for many these medications work well. It is impossible to know based on this one case if combining *Amanita* mushrooms and tricyclic antidepressants is harmful, but if so, the consequences are potentially very serious.

Other than the cases cited above, the negative physical effects of the mushrooms are reported to be short term and not serious. Research is needed to definitely determine the safety or risk of *Amanita muscaria* mushrooms and its cousins.

CHAPTER 2

THE CIA'S MAGIC BEANS:
*Anadenanthera peregrina/*Colubrina Seeds
(Yopo, Cohoba, Vilca, Cogioba, Kohobba)

Description and History

Anadenanthera peregrina and *Anadenanthera colubrina* are trees in the *Leguminosae* family of plants. Though theses trees are technically different species, their foliage, seeds, and habit are so alike that it is almost impossible for a layman to tell them apart. Both of these legumes produce seeds that are used to make a psychoactive snuff (powder for snorting).

The only way to tell the difference between the two species is the texture of the bark of the mature trees. *Anadenanthera colubrina* bark is smooth and dark while *Anadenanthera peregrina* bark is rough and brown/grayish with warts and lumps. *Anadenanthera peregrina* is also more sensitive to frost.

The use of *Anadenanthera peregrina* seeds as a mind-altering substance predates Columbus's discovery of the Americas in 1492. On Columbus's second journey to the Americas, approximately 1493–96, he observed the use of snuffs made from the seeds of *Anadenanthera peregrina*. Columbus described a "powder," which the "kings" of the Taino Indians of the island of Hispaniola would "snuff up," and that they would "lose consciousness and become like drunken men." Columbus decided to commission Friar Ramon Pane to study the customs of the Taino. Friar Pane described the practice of a shaman who "takes a certain powder called cohoba snuffing it up his nose, which intoxicates them so they do not know what they do."

In 1801, the explorer A. von Humboldt reported the use of yopo snuff by the Maypure Indians of Orinoco, and in the 1800s, the botanist Richard Spruce investigated use of yopo by the Guahibo Indians of the Orinoco basin, but his notes were not published until many years later.

In 1954, V. L. Stromberg isolated 5-hydroxy-N,N-dimethyltryptamine (5-OH-DMT) as a psychoactive chemical contained in *Anadenanthera peregrina* seeds. This chemical is also known as bufotenine, because it was first isolated from the venom of the *Bufo alavarius* toad (discussed in chapter 6 of this book). The following year, other scientists also identified N,N-dimethyltryptamine (DMT) as a psychoactive chemical contained in the seeds. Both bufotenine and DMT have little activity when snorted alone. Natives that use the *Anadenanthera peregrina* snuffs combine the seeds with limestone to make them psychoactive when snuffed.

I am skeptical of conspiracy theories and stories of the CIA performing secret studies on citizens of the United States. However, there is a large body of documentation regarding the United States Central Intelligence Agency's (CIA) use of yopo and bufotenine as part of mind-control experiments. These experiments were part of a CIA project started in the 1950s called MK-ULTRA. The project involved the use of many mind-altering drugs, and also the use of electronic signals to alter brain function. In 1977, Senator Ted Kennedy said with regards to MK-ULTRA that "the Deputy Director of the CIA revealed that over thirty universities and institutions were involved in an 'extensive testing and experimentation' program which included covert drug tests on unwitting citizens 'at all social levels, high and low, native Americans and foreign.' Several of these tests involved the administration of LSD to 'unwitting subjects in social situations.' At least one death, that of Dr. Olsen, resulted from these activities. The Agency itself acknowledged that these tests made little scientific sense. The agents doing the monitoring were not qualified scientific observers."

Dr. Frank Olsen was a U.S. Army biochemist and biological weapons researcher who was given LSD in 1953 as part of the CIA experiment. It is unclear whether or not he was told what he was given. He developed a "severe psychotic episode." The CIA reported that one week later Dr. Olsen committed suicide. The CIA doctor monitoring Olsen reported that the biochemist jumped out a tenth-floor window. Olsen's son disputes the report that his father committed suicide. He claims that his father was murdered because he had knowledge of sometimes-lethal interrogation techniques used by the CIA on Cold War prisoners. Frank Olsen's body was exhumed in 1994. It was concluded that cranial injuries had knocked Olsen unconscious prior to his ten-story plunge.

The MK-ULTRA program was started on the order of CIA director Allen Dulles, on April 13, 1953. It was headed by Dr.

Sidney Gottlieb. The project was largely a response to alleged mind-control techniques used by the Soviets, North Koreans, and the Chinese. The CIA was also interested in using such techniques to manipulate foreign leaders. In 1964, the project was renamed MKSEARCH. The project expanded to focus on producing a "truth serum" that could be used on Soviet spies.

The majority of MK-ULTRA records were destroyed in 1972 by order of CIA director Richard Helms. His decision limits the ability to fully investigate the more than 150 research projects sponsored by MK-ULTRA. Remaining CIA documents report that LSD was used in experiments with CIA employees, military personnel, doctors, other government agents, prostitutes, mentally ill patients, and members of the general public. These studies were often done without the subjects being informed of what they were being given. In 1955, as part of the MK-ULTRA experiments, H. S. Isbell administered yopo snuff and bufotenine to prisoners in the Lexington, Kentucky, federal narcotics farm. Oral and nasal dosages had little or no effect. Intramuscular dosages of 10 mg to 12.5 mg produced visual hallucinations and "a play of colors, lights, and patterns."

The MK-ULTRA activities of the CIA were first made public by the *New York Times* in December 1974. The revelation resulted in investigations by the U.S. Congress and a presidential commission known as the Rockefeller Commission. Though many of the records were destroyed in 1972, these investigations, along with an army investigation, revealed much information regarding MK-ULTRA.

Reports indicated that a large portion of the research involved the use of LSD. In one study, volunteers were given LSD for seventy-seven consecutive days. Researchers eventually concluded the effects of LSD were too unpredictable to be useful.

In addition to experiments using a number of substances, radiation was also explored as a method of mind control. In an experiment labeled Operation Midnight Climax, the CIA set up brothels with rooms that contained one-way mirrors and taping equipment. The purpose was to obtain a selection of men who would be too embarrassed to talk about what happened. Investigations revealed that Dr. Olsen's was not the only death resulting from the research. A professional tennis player in New York City, Harold Blaur, died as a result of an experiment with methylenedioxyamphetamine (MDA).

MDA is an illegal drug under Schedule I of the Controlled Substances Act of the United States. MDA is reported to have effects that are similar, though not identical, to methylenedioxymethamphetamine (MDMA). MDMA is the street drug commonly known as ecstasy.

It was revealed that studies were also carried out in Canada under MK-ULTRA. The studies were conducted under the direction of Dr. D. Ewen Cameron. In addition to studies using LSD, Dr. Cameron used various paralytic drugs and electroconvulsive therapy (ECT) at thirty to forty times the normal power. Cameron had developed a theory called "psychic driving." Based upon his theory, he placed subjects into a drug-induced coma from weeks to three months, while playing tape loops of noise or repetitive statements. Subjects for his experiments were usually individuals with relatively minor mental health problems, such as anxiety and postpartum depression. Many of them suffered long term from the effects of his experiments.

Anadenanthera peregrina/colubrina seeds are not controlled by the federal government. They are legal to possess, buy, sell, and cultivate. However, two of the chemicals contained in the seeds, bufotenine and DMT, are Schedule I under the Controlled Substances Act of the United States. This makes it illegal to possess, buy, sell, or produce bufotenine or DMT.

Typically the government has taken a hands-off approach to regulating the seeds, and there are many sources selling the seeds online. The government could at some future date attempt to regulate the seeds because of the chemicals they contain. Based upon the DEA's past history, they are more likely to interfere if they become aware of someone buying massive amounts of the seeds for extraction of illegal chemicals.

Chemistry and Physiological Effects

The two primary psychoactive chemicals in *Anadenanthera peregrina/colubrina* snuffs are bufotenine (5-OH-DMT) and DMT. This section will discuss the pharmacology and physiological effects of these two chemicals.

DMT is a white, pungent-smelling, crystalline solid. It is insoluble in water but soluble in organic solvents and aqueous acids. There is a lack of research on how DMT causes its effects. The DMT molecule is similar to the neurotransmitter serotonin, and it is likely that it hits several of the same sites as serotonin does. However, more research is needed. Dilated pupils, hypertension (high blood pressure), and increased heart rate are common physiological effects. It has a half-life in the blood of about fifteen minutes.

Bufotenine (5-OH-DMT) is a tryptamine related to the neurotransmitter serotonin. Despite many years of its use, there is still little information regarding how it has its effects on the brain and body.

How People Obtain and Use
Anadenanthera peregrina/Colubrina Seeds

DMT and bufotenine (5-OH-DMT) must be combined with another substance to increase their activity when taken nasally. Traditionally, limestone was used for this purpose. In modern times, baking soda is most often used in its place. Because *Anadenanthera peregrina* and *Anadenanthera colubrine* are different species, it is possible that the psychoactive chemicals in their seeds may have some differences. However, both types of seeds have been used for the snuffs.

There is some evidence that indigenous people may have sometimes added *Banisteriopsis caapi,* the common ayahuasca ingredient that will be described in a later chapter, to *Anadenanthera* snuffs. *Banisteriopsis caapi* contains a monoamine oxidase inhibitor (MAOI). Subjective reports of *Anadenanthera* seed use have indicated that the addition of an MAOI enhanced and prolonged the experience.

The seeds can be purchased online by typing something like "anadenanthera seeds buy" into a search engine. Following are a few online sources:

www.giftsfromtheancients.com
www.bouncingbearbotanicals.com
www.psychoactiveherbs.com
www.shamanhut.com

People use the seeds by either snuffing or smoking them. Regardless of how they use them, they start by placing the seeds in a pan and heating them until the outer skin puffs up. A typical dose is about three seeds per person. After removing the seeds from the pan and letting them cool, the outer skin is removed. Next, the inner white seed is combined with some baking soda in a coffee grinder. The combination is three parts seed to one part baking soda. The mixture is ground into a fine powder. The powder is then either inhaled with a straw through the nose or heated in a pipe and inhaled.

Those who are willing to wait for years to harvest the seeds can grow their own *Anadenanthera peregrina* or *Anadenanthera colubrina* trees. Both types of *Anadenthera* are grown in the same way. One should make sure that the seeds used are described by the seller as viable. If such seeds cannot be found, tell your supplier that you intend to grow the trees and ask for the most recently picked seeds. Many of the seeds sold for psychoactive use are too old to germinate. Fresh seeds will germinate within a few days, while most old seeds will never grow. The seeds should first be presoaked in sterilized water for twenty-four hours. If you cannot find sterilized water, or if you do not want to buy sterilized water, then tap water can be boiled for several minutes and then allowed to cool to room temperature.

The seeds are then placed in a growing medium that does

not contain any organic matter. Seeds should be placed about one centimeter below the surface. The soil should be kept damp, but not wet, until the seeds sprout. They should be kept warm. Someone has suggested a temperature between approximately 22°C and 26°C (71.6°F to 78.8°F). It should take a week or less for them to sprout. The soil should be allowed to dry between waterings. As the seedlings grow, they will like a well-draining soil and a sunny, warm environment. Their pots may need to be changed if they outgrow them.

The *Anadenanthera perigrina*/Colubrina Seed Experience

Smoking or snorting *Anadenanthera* seed preparations results in a rapid onset of effects of within about a minute. Most reports indicate that snorting *Anadenanthera* results in more intense effects than smoking. The initial effects tend to be somewhat stimulating and last twenty to forty minutes. The latter part of the experience is typically more sedating. Visual hallucinations are a prominent part of the experience. Some individuals who have inhaled DMT describe the experience of using *Anadenanthera* as similar but less intense. Light often takes on multiple colors and rainbow effects are often seen. Closing the eyes will result in intense visual experiences. Feelings of pressure in the head and face are often reported. Flushing of the face and watering of the eyes is common. Nausea and vomiting are a commonly reported part of the experience. If the seed is snorted, nasal discomfort and watering is typical. Loss of coordination and the desire to move one's arms and legs is sometimes experienced.

Athlete on Anadenanthera peregrina/*Colubrina Seeds*

"The very first thing I noticed was a physical effect. It felt kind of like a pressure or squeezing of my body. In a little while it seemed that some of my muscles were beginning to tighten. These body effects seemed to be decreased when I began to notice changes in my vision. I am not sure whether the physical effects changed, or if I just lost focus on them when my focus changed to the visual effects. Lights became intense, and I went from avoiding light to wanting to gaze at the light, which produced weird patterns, kind of like what happens when you press on your eyes when they are closed. I forget what that is called. Is it phosphene activity? I then slipped into a much more intense experience. I had all kinds of intense visual experiences. Colors were altered and became intense. Closing my eyes also resulted in intense visual effects. This was so much that closing my eyes was unpleasant. After a long time, the intense effects decreased, leaving me with a very pleasant feeling of thoughtfulness and meditation. It was this after-effect that was most enjoyable and beneficial. In the future I will try a lower dose to see if I can go right to this latter point."

Some Risks of Using *Anadenanthera peregrina/*Colubrina Seeds

There is little information regarding the risks of using *Anadenanthera* seeds. They do not appear to be addictive. Hypersensitivity or allergy is always possible, but unlikely. The worst effects that most people experience are vomiting, headaches, throat discomfort, and nasal pain. Also, as with any substance, individuals with psychological problems should avoid this and other mind-altering substances. Use of these seeds can result in impaired coordination, judgment, and slowed physical responses. For this reason, use of them while driving or doing any other task that requires physical ability or judgment should be avoided. Obviously, driving under the influence of *Anadenanthera* seeds would present a great danger to the user and to others.

CHAPTER 3

GIFT FROM THE GREEN FAIRY:
Artemisia absinthium
(Absinthe, Wormwood, Grand Wormwood, Absinthe Wormwood)

Description and History

Artemisia absinthium is a perennial, herbaceous plant, with a woody root called a rhizome. It is native to Europe, Asia, and northern Africa. Its straight stems grow to a height of approximately one to three feet. Its leaves are greenish-gray on top and whitish-green on the bottom, with white or silver hairs.

It flowers from summer to early fall. The flowers are light yellow.

The plant is common in the wild and can be easily cultivated. It can be propagated by seeds or cuttings. It grows best in dry, nitrogen-rich soil. It is not native to North America, but it has been naturalized there. It has a distinct odor, which appears to help it resist pests.

The name artemesia comes from the name for the Greek god Artemis. The name absinthium probably derives from an ancient Greek word meaning "bitter," or "undrinkable." The plant *Artemisia absinthium* has become more commonly known as wormwood. This name may come from the Anglo-Saxon word "wermode," which means roughly "mind pre-server." This title is probably due to the plant's mind-altering properties. The name wormwood may likely have stuck due to the plant's historical use as a treatment for internal parasites like worms.

The earliest known mention of the use of *Artemisia absinthium* may be from an ancient Egyptian document written in 1500 BC, known as the Ebers Papyrus. The papyrus notes the use of the plant as a treatment for intestinal parasites.

The ancient Greeks dedicated the plant to the goddess Artemis, a major Greek goddess. She was born as the result of an affair between Zeus and Apollo's twin sister Leto. Artemis was the goddess of the wilderness, forest, hills, wild animals, hunters, and hunting. In ancient Greek art she was typically shown with a bow and arrow, a crescent moon over her head, and accompanied by a deer.

The ancient Greek writer Hippocrates described wormwood as a common part of medical treatment. Wormwood was prescribed for the treatment of jaundice, rheumatism, anemia, and menstrual cramps. The Greeks also considered it useful as an antidote to the poisons of certain mushrooms, hemlock, and even the occasional sea dragon. At various times, wormwood has been used as a remedy for upset stomach, other digestive problems, poor appetite, a sedative, to bring on childbirth more quickly, and to expel the afterbirth.

The Old Testament of the Bible makes several references to wormwood. Deuteronomy 29:18 says, "Lest there should be among you man, or woman, or family, or tribe, whose heart turneth away this day from the Lord our God, to go and serve the gods of these nations; lest there should be among you a root that beareth gall and wormwood." In modern language, this means something like: God has made a deal with you so that you would not worship any other gods, and so that none of your plants would be poisonous or bitter.

In Jeremiah 9:15, the Bible says, "Therefore thus saith the Lord of hosts, the God of Israel; Behold, I will feed them, even this people, with wormwood, and give them gall to drink." In this section, the God of Israel is saying he will feed them (i.e., false prophets or liars) something really bitter and poisonous.

The reference to wormwood in the Bible that has resulted in the largest amount of discussion is in the Book of Revelation in the New Testament. In the Book of Revelation 8:10–11, it is stated, "And the third angel sounded, and there fell a great star from heaven, burning as it were a lamp, and it fell upon the third part of the rivers, and upon the fountains of water; And the name of the star is called Wormwood: and the third part of the waters became wormwood; and many men died of the waters, because they were made bitter." The Book of Revelation then goes on to say that parts of the sun, moon, and stars become dark, and then a bunch of bad stuff starts to happen. Many people have interpreted the reference to wormwood as a star falling from the sky to mean that a large meteor will hit Earth. Some have interpreted the use of wormwood in the Book of Revelation to symbolically refer to the bitterness that will be widespread at the end of the world.

In addition to its use by gods and its medical uses, wormwood has been used as an insect repellant and mixed in to potpourri. It has been used in beer as a replacement for hops.

Hops provide the bitterness to beer, and wormwood's bitter flavor can work as a reasonable substitute. It has been used in the liquor vermouth.

Absinthe

The most famous beverage made from wormwood is absinthe.

Absinthe is a highly alcoholic, distilled spirit that contains wormwood as a primary ingredient. It is also typically flavored with anise and fennel. Many other herbs are sometimes used for flavor, including hyssop, star anise, coriander, juniper, and nutmeg.

Absinthe most often has a light green color, but a clear variety is also made. The green color is usually the result of some of the herbs used to flavor it, but it is sometimes artificially colored. It traditionally contains 60 to 75 percent alcohol, or 120- to 150-proof.

There are different styles of absinthe produced, including Blanche, Verte, and Absenta.

- *Blanche* is a clear absinthe that contains the distilled oils only of the wormwood and other herbs that it is initially distilled with.
- *Verte,* meaning green in French, is green in color, resulting from the herbs being steeped in it after the initial fermentation.
- *Absenta* is a Spanish variety that is usually sweeter and has a slight citrus flavor.

An elaborate ritual surrounds the traditional serving of absinthe. It has been said that the ritual is more enjoyable than the actual drink. Water and sugar are mixed with absinthe, probably to make its bitter taste more palatable. The absinthe is poured into the glass first. Special glasses that have a small bubble in the bottom are traditionally used to allow the pourer to easily measure the amount of absinthe to be poured. Absinthe is poured until it reaches the top of the bubble, which serves as a fill line. A specially made slotted spoon, often resembling a small pie server, is placed on the top of the glass. A single sugar cube is then placed on top of the spoon. Water is then poured over the sugar cube, through the slots in the spoon, into the glass, dissolving the sugar cube as it pours, and filling the glass while everything is mixed together.

The creation of absinthe has been historically credited to Dr. Pierre Ordinaire in 1789, though his credit may be more a myth than a reality. The French doctor was reportedly trained in both medicine and pharmacology. At the time, he was living in the Swiss town of Couvet, in the Canton of Neuchatel. He had chosen to leave his original home for what was described as political reasons. He discovered wormwood while traveling in Val-de-Travers, and subsequently mixed it with alcohol and other herbs to produce a potion containing 68 percent alcohol.

For some reason he was inspired to use this potion, nicknamed "la Fee Verte" (the Green Fairy), on many of his sick patients. Many reports were made of its miraculous healing powers, and it came to be described as a cure for all ills.

After the death of the doctor, his secret potion was supposedly passed on to Mademoiselle Grande-Pierre, and then to the Henroid sisters in Couvet. Some believe that the sisters may have already been using the potion before the arrival of the doctor.

Either way, the sisters developed a successful business selling the Green Fairy. In 1797, they sold the recipe for the potion to a Major Dubied. The major, along with his son Macellin and his son-in-law Henri-Louis Pernod, built the first commercial absinthe distillery. They located their operation in Couvet and named it Dubied Pere et Fils.

The absinthe business proved to be very successful and they soon expanded. Their business eventually grew to the point of producing 30,000 liters per day and shipping it to much of the world.

In the 1840s, absinthe was given to French troops as a treatment for malaria. They brought their desire for the drink back with them to France. Absinthe became increasingly popular in the early to mid-1800s, moving it from a cure-all to a spirit that was imbibed simply for pleasure.

In the 1880s, mass production of absinthe became possible, resulting in a significant decrease in price along with a further jump in its popularity. By 1910, the French alone were consuming 36 million liters of the stuff, more than their annual wine consumption!

Absinthe's popularity moved well beyond Europe. The Old Absinthe House, christened the Absinthe Room in 1847, was originally built in New Orleans in 1807, where it still stands. Check out their website at www.oldabsinthehouse.com.

Many famous artists and writers have described their love of absinthe. There are several classic paintings with absinthe content. Oscar Wilde wrote much about his fondness of the liquor, including, "What difference is there between a glass of absinthe and a sunset?" Ernest Hemingway and Vincent van Gogh were well known for their love of absinthe. Even the famous British occultist Aleister Crowley wrote a lyrical essay dedicated to it, titled "Absinthe: The Green Goddess."

Despite its popularity, or perhaps because of it, the absinthe trade would come to a sudden halt in the early 1900s. The combination of a popular temperance movement involving all alcoholic beverages, some sensational press reports of atrocious crimes committed by individuals reputed to have used absinthe, and exaggerated concerns about the effects of wormwood on the brain resulted in absinthe being banned throughout much of the world. In the beginning of the twentieth century, many countries began to ban alcohol, including the United States by 1920.

On August 28, 1905, Jean Lanfrey murdered his pregnant wife and two daughters after consuming a small amount of absinthe. The murder occurred in Switzerland, but with the help of the massive European prohibition movement, "The Absinthe Murder" was widely reported throughout the world. The fact that Lanfrey had consumed only two ounces of absinthe, along with seven glasses of wine, six glasses of cognac, a coffee with brandy, and two crème de menthes, did not prevent the absinthe from being identified as the culprit. With all of this alcohol on board, he reportedly got into an argument with his wife and asked her to polish his shoes. When she refused, he retrieved a rifle, shot her in the head, and then went after and shot his four-year-old and two-year-old daughters. He dragged his wife's dead body out to the garden and passed out. He was convicted of the three murders in a one-day trial. A psychologist argued that he suffered from "absinthe madness" when he committed the murders. His intoxicated state allowed him to receive a thirty-year prison sentence and avoid the death penalty.

Concerns about the effects of absinthe on the brain were raised in the 1800s and early 1900s. Doctors had noticed that chronic, heavy users of absinthe sometimes developed tremors, convulsions, hallucinations, insomnia, and even died. They labeled this combination of symptoms as absinthism.

Subsequent studies on rats showed that very high doses of thujones, the primary psychoactive chemicals in wormwood, could induce convulsions. Other researchers strongly debated the conclusion that wormwood or thujones were harmful to the brain. The symptoms observed in chronic users of absinthe were identical to those developed by chronic alcoholics who did not drink absinthe. It was also pointed out that the amount of thujones needed to cause rat hallucinations was much greater than what one could get from absinthe.

Concerns about absinthe, and alcohol in general, would lead to laws banning the sale of absinthe as early as 1898. Belgium and Brazil banned its sale in 1906, and Switzerland followed the next year. The United States outlawed its sale in 1912 and France in 1915. The mass banning of absinthe resulted in its near demise until the 1990s.

In the 1990s, British businessman George Rowley realized that despite absinthe being banned in much of the world, Britain had never actually passed a law banning the sale or production of the drink. In 1998, he opened the Bohemia Beer House, later named BBH Spirits, and began selling absinthe on a large scale in Britain. Rowley's actions resulted in what has been called the "absinthe revival." Re-examination of the old medical opinions resulted in the recognition that concerns about the dangers of absinthe were mostly unfounded.

Absinthe is now legal in most of the world. However, Europe and the United States have laws regulating the amount of thujones that can be present in absinthe. European law limits the amount of thujones to 35 mg per liter of absinthe. The U.S. FDA makes it illegal to sell any product meant for human consumption that contains thujones from *Artemisia absinthium*. The FDA also makes it illegal to import any food or liquor that contains *Artemisia absinthium*. The US has recently allowed the sales and importation of varieties of absinthe that contain less than 10 mg of thujones per kg of the substance.

The U.S. laws leave some confusion as to what exactly is legal to import or sell. Everyone seems to agree that possession of absinthe is legal no matter what. It is just the commerce of it that is an issue. Foreign companies that ship absinthe to the United States all seem to deny any problems having their products get through customs.

As already stated, the primary psychoactive substances in wormwood are the thujones, specifically alpha-thujone and beta-thujone. Thujone in its two stereoisomeric forms (alpha/beta) is a ketone and monoterpine, with a boiling point of 201°C and a molecular weight of 152.24. The thujones occur naturally in several plants besides wormwood, including some junipers, mugwort, and sage.

Chemistry and Physiological Effects

The thujones have been the only psychoactive chemicals identified in wormwood. It was once thought that thujones produced their effects by action upon the same receptors as THC, the primary psychoactive chemical in marijuana. Research has since shown that this belief was false.

Studies have demonstrated that the thujones act as antagonists at gamma-aminobutyric acid (GABA) type A receptor sites in the brain. GABA is active in suppressing convulsions/seizures. It is hypothesized that antagonism of GABA is the cause of convulsions seen in rats given high dosages of thujones.

Thujones also act as antagonists at 5-hydroxytryptamine-3 (5-HT-3) receptors, a subtype of serotonin receptors. This 5-HT-3 receptor activity is probably also a cause of the psychoactive effects of thujones.

The metabolism of the thujones occurs primarily in the liver.

How People Obtain and Use *Artemisia absinthium*

Sources for *Artemisia absinthium* (wormwood) can be easily found by going online and typing into any search engine "buy wormwood." The site www.iamshaman.com sells dried wormwood, concentrated wormwood extracts, wormwood oil, and powdered wormwood. This site also lists for sale complete kits for making a homemade version of absinthe. Other sources for wormwood products:

www.giftsfromtheancients.com
www.psychoactiveherbs.com
www.shamanhut.com

The two ways people use *Artemisia absinthium* (wormwood), aside from making absinthe, are to smoke it or take it orally. Browsing the available research did not result in any clear information regarding the amount of the psychoactive chemicals that enter the bloodstream by smoking or ingesting wormwood. The amount of thujones present in different samples of wormwood also varies. This makes it difficult to know exactly what doses lead to what effects.

Whether smoking or ingesting wormwood orally, most consumers of wormwood recommend starting with the lowest dose and then increasing the dose later if one wishes. Given the fact that high doses of thujones can cause convulsions and other problems, starting slow would be the best policy.

Wormwood can be smoked in a pipe or rolled in papers. Most extracts can also be smoked. Most wormwood users start with one bowl or one-half of a rolled joint, and then smoke more if desired.

To take wormwood orally, the extracts, oils, and powder can be mixed with some liquid or placed in capsules. A common starting dose of an extract or concentrated form is one teaspoon. It is usually mixed with a strong flavored liquid, like some kind of alcohol or juice, to moderate the bitter flavor.

Wormwood foliage can be used to make a tea by adding it to boiling water and filtering it. Some lemon juice added to the tea helps with the taste a little. About two tablespoons is a common amount of wormwood to start with when brewing tea.

Absinthe can now be found in some liquor stores. Typing "buy absinthe" into any Internet search engine will also yield many sources. Some good online sites for absinthe:

www.originalabsinthe.com
www.absinthesupply.net
www.absinth.com

The oldest online source for absinthe is www.eabsinthe.com. Eabsinthe is the online arm of BBH Spirits, the company credited with starting the modern "absinthe revival." They are located in Britain. A very unique absinthe site is the Virtual Absinthe Museum Web Shop, located online at www.oxygenee.com/vintage.html, which sells bottles of pre-prohibition absinthe bottled from 1915 and earlier. Most of these sites sell traditional absinthe-serving items, like glasses and spoons. Absinthe can be drunk straight, but sugar and water are usually added.

A type of pseudo-absinthe can also be made at home. True absinthe is made by including wormwood in the distillation process. This likely reduces the bitterness somewhat and imparts a specific character to the liquor. Something very similar to absinthe can be made by combining an already distilled spirit with wormwood, and then adding other flavorings. This results in a product that differs only slightly from the real thing. Vodka or Everclear (151 proof grain alcohol) are used as the liquor, because they have no flavor besides the alcohol. Here are a couple of recipes.

Absinthe Recipe 1

Combine one pint of vodka (or Everclear for a more potent drink) with two tablespoons of dried, crumbled wormwood, and place it in a glass container with a lid. Let the mixture sit for about two days. You might want to swirl the container around once or twice per day to mix everything up. After the two days, strain the mixture with a fine mesh strainer (a coffee filter will probably also do) and return the liquid to the container. Add one tablespoon anise seeds, one teaspoon mint leaves, and one-half teaspoon coriander seeds to the container. Crushing the seeds a little (not grinding) will help them to release their flavor, but it is not essential. Cover the container again and let it sit for about seven days. Then filter the contents through a coffee filter. Enjoy your homemade absinthe.

Absinthe Recipe 2

Combine a pint of vodka or Everclear in a container with two tablespoons of dried, crushed wormwood and cover it with a lid. Let it sit for two days and then strain it. Return the liquid to the container and add two teaspoons fennel or anise seeds, two teaspoons dried angelica root, one-half teaspoon coriander seeds, and four whole cardamon pods. Let this sit for about a week and then filter using a coffee filter. Serve in the traditional way. The base of two tablespoons of wormwood and one pint of vodka or Everclear can be used with a variety of additives for flavoring.

The *Artemisia absinthium* Experience

Smoking an extract will produce a stronger effect than plain wormwood. Reports of the effects of smoking wormwood or its extract vary significantly. This may be due to differences in thujone content, individual physical differences, mental set, or something else.

On the less intense end, smoking results in some relaxation and calming of the mind. In addition to this effect, many people report feeling more alert and slightly stimulated, though this is not consistent. Sensations of feeling physically relaxed and heaviness in the body are also common.

Those who report a more intense experience often describe it as similar to a marijuana buzz or the effects of taking a moderate amount of an opiate, such as vicodin. Users typically then go on to state that the experience is not exactly like that of using either of these substances. The onset of the experience is usually within thirty seconds to one minute, with a duration of about thirty minutes.

Ingesting wormwood produces mental effects similar to those of smoking, along with the range from mild to fairly intense effects. A big difference between oral ingestion and smoking is that the extreme bitterness becomes an important factor. The taste of wormwood makes it difficult to ingest rapidly and it can also wreak havoc on a person's stomach. It sometimes leads to nausea severe enough to cause regurgitation.

Oral ingestion also takes longer to cause an effect and the effect typically lasts longer. The onset of the effect is typically twenty to thirty minutes, with a duration of one and a half to two hours.

One consideration in how to use wormwood is that the delayed onset of oral ingestion makes it difficult to know if one has taken too much until it is too late. The rapid onset of the effects of smoking wormwood tells users when they have taken enough. Most people take wormwood orally with no difficulties, but given that high doses of wormwood can cause problems, an alternate method of use is worth considering.

The effects of absinthe are similar to the effects of drinking any hard alcohol. The low amount of thujones in most modern absinthe, especially in the United States, reduces or eliminates the unique effects of the drink. Making your own absinthe allows you to alter the amount of wormwood and the corresponding thujones. When the wormwood content has an effect on people, some report that it intensifies the effects of just the alcohol alone. It is sometimes reported that despite feeling the intoxicating effects of alcohol, the user's mind is not as clouded. Some users also report feeling relaxed but not lethargic.

Skeptic Scientist Smokes Wormwood

"I prepared and smoked one bowl of flaked *Artemisia absinthium*. I took five or six hits; I forget. I was kind of skeptical given how cheap it was to buy. My doubts were quickly dispersed, however. By the first or second hit, I was definitely feeling an effect. I tried to relate it to something. Maybe vicodin or a couple of codeine. My legs felt relaxed, my arms felt relaxed, and my neck felt relaxed. I leaned my head against the wall behind my bed. It seemed weird that having my head pressed directly against the wall did not seem uncomfortable. On the contrary, it was a pleasurable experience. There was definitely a bitter aftertaste, making me wonder what it would be like to drink the stuff. At first the harshness of the smoke on my throat made me think I would not take more than two hits, but once the more euphoric feeling came on, I was craving more. The bitter aftertaste seemed to increase, so I got some punch out of the refrigerator and drank it. This helped with the taste. I just laid back, relaxed, and watched some television. After about thirty or forty minutes I felt back to normal and the effects had subsided."

Some Risks of Using *Artemesia absinthium*

Using wormwood has many of the same basic risks as the use of any mind-altering substance. People could get intoxicated and do something stupid. People can get addicted. People could drive while impaired and hurt themselves or others. Use of absinthe brings with it all of the additional potential problems associated with the use of any kind of alcohol.

Aside from these and other general risks of using substances, the two risks that have been reported as specific to wormwood (or wormwood products) use are negative effects on the brain and negative effects on the liver.

Wormwood's Negative Effects on the Brain

The potential for negative mental effects were noted a long time ago and played a major part in the banning of absinthe in the early twentieth century. Since the ban, there has been a lot of debate about whether absinthe causes problems with brain function that are beyond those simply caused by heavy alcohol use.

The literature on absinthe/wormwood and the brain contains a lot of poor research, flawed reasoning, and fear. There is also some good research and solid thinking. To cover this entire area would require several chapters. However, reviewing most of this literature allows one to draw a couple of conclusions:

1. Thujones, which are contained in varying quantities in wormwood and absinthe, in large doses can produce convulsions in some lab creatures. Case examples of people who have ingested large amounts of thujones indicate that large doses of thujones can probably induce convulsions in humans.
2. It is likely that along with these seizures, high dosages of thujones carry a risk of death. There have been no research studies indicating what the dangerous dosage of thujones would be in humans.

Studies on rats have shown that a dose of thujones causing convulsions is between approximately 12.5 mg/kg and 35.5 mg/kg. This means that at 12.5 mg/kg, no rats had convulsions, and that at 35.5 mg/kg, all rats had convulsions. Studies of the lethal dose of thujones indicated an approximate average lethal dose of 45 mg/kg, with no rats dying at 30 mg/kg and all rats dying by 60 mg/kg.

How similar the effects on rats are to the effects on humans is still unknown. Based upon the rat studies, if a rat was the same as a human, the amount of thujones that would cause convulsions in a human weighing 80 kg (176 pounds) would range between approximately 1,000 mg (1 gram) and 2,840 mg. In other words, a 1,000-mg dose would be the highest amount to not produce convulsions in humans, and a 2,840-mg dose would cause convulsions in all humans. The rat study–based lethal dose for an 80-kg human would average 3,600 mg, with the highest nonlethal dose being 2,400 mg, and the dose at which we all would die being 4,800 mg.

In reviewing information on the Internet regarding the

convulsive and lethal dosages of thujones for humans based on rat studies, several sites seemed to have confused milligrams and grams. It appeared that somewhere an error was made and many other people just quoted the same wrong figures. The result was that the dosage information was off by 1,000 times. Luckily, the error was made on the side of safety, making it seem that the lethal/convulsive dose was 1,000 times less than what it really is.

Historical recipes that have been tested for thujone content have resulted in ranges of 2 mg to 10 mg per liter of absinthe. The European Union currently limits the amount of thujones in absinthe to 35 mg per kg, and the United States limits thujone content in absinthe to 10 mg per kg. A liter of absinthe weighs almost exactly 1 kg.

It can be seen from these figures that the amount of thujones contained in historical or modern absinthe is well below that determined to cause convulsions or death. This leads further credence to the opinion that the medical problems blamed on absinthe were most likely due to the alcohol content and not wormwood.

Many samples of wormwood taken from many parts of the world have been examined for essential oil content and thujone content. Thujones are contained entirely in the essential oils. By determining the amount of essential oil in a wormwood sample and then determining the percentage of thujones in the oil, one can determine the amount and percentage of thujones in the wormwood sample.

Examination of wormwood samples have resulted in oil percentages ranging from 0.3 percent to 1.6 percent, with an average of 0.6 percent. Thujone content in the essential oils ranged from none detected (0 percent) to 70.6 percent. By taking these averages, the average amount of thujones present in wormwood would be 0.1 percent. The minimal amount of thujones would be 0 percent with a theoretical maximum of 1.12 percent. Though it is theoretically possible to have a thujone content of 1.12 percent, the largest found was actually 0.45 percent.

These percentages mean that 1 kg of wormwood would contain an average of 1 g (1,000 mg) of thujones. The lowest amount of thujones in wormwood would of course be none or 0 g, with the theoretically highest possible amount of thujones being 11.2 g, and the highest amounts of thujones identified in a sample being 4.5 g. Wormwood extracts and wormwood oils would obviously contain significantly higher amounts of thujones.

This should allow the reader to make some general comparisons to the convulsant/lethal amounts of thujones present in a sample of wormwood or wormwood product. With regards to risk of harm, it is obvious that the extracts and oils contain the greatest risk for overdose.

Wormwood's Negative Effects on the Liver

The second most common concern raised about possible harm from *Artemisia absinthium* is the possibility of liver damage. This concern seems odd, because a huge body of alternative medicine and herbal treatment literature recommends it being used to protect the liver. This literature often reports that the extreme bitterness of the herb stimulates all of the organs involved in the digestive system and the removal of waste products. It is also reported to increase bile production in the liver. Studies in rats have also shown that wormwood can prevent the liver-damaging effects of acetaminophen and other chemicals toxic to the liver.

So where does the notion of wormwood being harmful to the liver come from? On reviewing the literature, I was able to find only one study that reported liver damage from wormwood use. This case has been reported over and over again as support that wormwood damages the liver. The reason for the popularity of this study is probably because it was published in a highly respected journal, the *New England Journal of Medicine* (*NEJM*).

The article by Steven D. Weisbord, Jeremy B. Soule, and Paul L. Kimmel, published September 1997, reported "acute renal failure (i.e., sudden liver failure)" of a thirty-one-year-old male after ingesting a large amount (approximately 10 ml) of wormwood oil. His father found him at home agitated, incoherent, and in a disoriented state. Paramedics described tonic and clonic seizures. In the hospital he was lethargic but belligerent. Emergency physicians injected him with haloperidol (haldol), which got rid of his convulsions and his acting out. Tests indicated severe liver problems.

After being hospitalized and a follow-up in the community, he had no further problems. The doctors concluded that because they could find no other explanation for his liver problems and because he had taken a large amount of wormwood oil, that wormwood oil in high doses can lead to severe liver problems.

So what can one conclude about the effects of wormwood on the liver? Currently there are no studies that determine what exactly are the effects of wormwood on the liver. There is a small possibility that it could affect the liver negatively, but this is unlikely. It is my hope that future research will clarify this issue.

CHAPTER 4

THE SHAMAN'S POTION:
Ayahuasca
(Yage, Huasca, Daime, Caapi)

Description and History

Ayahuasca potions have been used by South American natives for hundreds of years. At least seventy separate groups of indigenous people that use ayahuasca have been identified. These people live in Brazil, Venezuela, Colombia, Ecuador, Peru, and Bolivia. Ayahuasca has been called by more than forty different names. The first written accounts of ayahuasca use were made about 150 years ago. These pioneering reports were recorded by Manuel Villavicencio and Richard Spruce.

Richard Spruce was a former schoolteacher and botanist from Britain. In 1851, he discovered that a group of natives living in the Amazon were imbibing a mind-altering potion they called "caapi." Spruce ingested the caapi potion and took part in the group's ritual. He also found specimens of one of the plants the beverage was prepared from.

Over the next several years, Spruce encountered groups using similar potions in Venezuela and Ecuador. In 1858, an Ecuadorian civil servant named Manuel Villavicencio described the effects of using caapi, but he called the drink "ayahuasca," the Quecha word for "the vine of the souls." While on ayahuasca, Villavicencio experienced himself as flying to incredible places. He described how the natives used ayahuasca to obtain information on how to battle their enemies and how to help their sick relatives.

Several other explorers that came after Spruce and Villavicencio described the use of ayahuasca. A film of ayahuasca ceremonies was shown at the annual meeting of the American Pharmaceutical Association in 1923.

In 1930, a new religion based around the use of ayahuasca was founded. The religion, called Santo Daime, was founded by Raimundo Irineu Serra. His followers refer to him as Master Irineu. Irineu was a Brazilian rubber-tapper born in 1902. In 1922, he migrated to the Amazonian rainforest, where the rubber trade was thriving. He had been raised as a Catholic, but his time in the Amazon brought him into contact with the Peruvian natives that lived there. They introduced Irineu to their native beliefs, and to the use of ayahuasca.

While using ayahuasca, Irineu had visions of a "Divine Lady, sitting in the moon." She told him to go into the forest for eight days and drink ayahuasca. While using ayahuasca in the forest, he saw a spirit he called the "Queen of the Forest," whom he associated with the Virgin Mary. The Queen of the Forest told him to found a new religion based upon the sacrament of ayahuasca. Santo Daime translates as "the holy give me herb." Irineu reportedly channeled many hymns, which are the church's guiding principles.

Many of the beliefs of Santo Daime are Christian, but they

also include ideas of reincarnation and the importance of protecting the rainforest. The Queen of the Forest is worshipped as a teacher. The hymns from Irineu are considered as another Gospel of Christ. One part of a common hymn goes "Daime forca, daime amor, daime luz," which translates as "Give me strength, give me love, give me light." Ayahuasca is taken as a sacrament, and the experiences it produces serve as the most important teacher. One of their rituals involves taking ayahuasca several times over a twelve-hour period. During this time, members dance a specified formation and rhythm intended to create a specific current of energy.

Irineu died in 1971 and leadership of the church passed to one of his principal followers, Sebastiao Mota de Melo, known as Padrinho Sebastiao. Sebastiao died in 1990, leaving the church in the hands of his son, Alfredo Gregorio de Melo. The Brazilian Federal Drug Council investigated the group over concerns about their use of the mind-altering substance ayahuasca and reports of cult brain washing. Their report concluded that the group posed no danger, and it actually praised the church for the positive effects it had on many of its followers. Today, the Santo Daime church has expanded beyond Brazil, to such places as the United States, Japan, Spain, Holland, Austria, Germany, Italy, and France. Their churches have many sites on the Web. Just type "Santo Daime" into any search engine for a listing.

In addition to Santo Daime, two other religious movements have been inspired by the use of ayahuasca, Uniao do Vegetal (UDV) and Barquinia. The UDV, which is called in English the Union of the Vegetable Beneficent Spiritist Center, was founded in 1961 by another rubber-tapper named Jose Gabriel da Costa. Mestre Gabriel, as he was called by his followers, had his first ayahuasca experiences with natives in Bolivia.

UDV members participate in the ritual use of ayahuasca at least twice a month. Their teachings are Christian based, but they also incorporate a focus on nature. The UDV claims to have over 6,000 members. Barquinia is the smallest of the three ayahuasca-inspired religions. It is an off-shoot of Santo Daime. It was founded by Daniel Pereira de Matos.

Many different ingredients have been used to make ayahuasca. However, all ayahuasca potions contain two essential ingredients. The first is a plant or seed containing a monoamine oxidase inhibitor (MAOI), most commonly the vine *Banisteriopsis caapi*. The second is a plant containing the natural hallucinogenic N,N-Dimethyltryptamine (DMT), most commonly leaves of *Psychotria viridis* (also called chacruna).

These two essential ingredients used separately have little or no psychoactive effect when taken orally. When DMT is taken orally, it is broken down by the body, eliminating its psychoactive effects. However, when a plant or seed containing a MAOI is used with the DMT-containing plant, the DMT is not broken down and it remains psychoactive. It is noteworthy that groups of indigenous peoples were able to discover this complex effect.

Banisteriopsis caapi is a vine that grows wild in the Amazon. Several alkaloids have been identified from *Banisteriopsis caapi*. The most significant for ayahuasca use are harmine, harmaline, and *d*-leptaflorine (also called tetrahydroharmine). These alkaloids are MAOIs, and they, along with others, are referred to generally as harmala alkaloids. By inhibiting the activity of MAO, these MAOIs allow DMT to be psychoactive when taken orally. *Psychotria viridis* is an Amazonian plant that has leaves containing significant levels of DMT. Though *Banisteriopsis caapi* and *Psychotria viridis* are the most common plants used to make ayahuasca, any plant containing a MAOI can be combined with any plant containing DMT to make it. Because there are many such plants, ayahuasca potions are made with many different ingredients.

The other commonly used MAOI in ayahuasca is syrian rue seed (technically known as peganum harmala seed). These seeds contain about 2 percent harmala alkaloids, which is more than any other plant material. For this reason, many makers of ayahuasca prefer them to *Banisteriopsis caapi*. Some ayahuasca aficionados report that the nature of the experience is somehow different when syrian rue seeds are used instead of *Banisteriopsis caapi*. This is possible because the two ingredients contain other alkaloids that differ from each other and may contribute to differences in their psychoactive effects. It is also possible that any differences are due to the expectations of the users and not actual differences in the MAOI material used.

Besides *Psychotria viridis,* other DMT-containing plants that can be used in ayahuasca are *Acacia madenii* (maiden's wattle), *Desmanthus illinoensis* (bundle flower), *Diplopterys cabrerana* (chagro-panga), *Mimosa hostilis* (jurema), and phalaris grass (reed canary grass). There are at least a hundred other DMT-containing plants, but those listed here are some of the most commonly available.

Acacia madenii is a medium-size tree that grows wild in many areas. The bark of the tree is used. It contains 0.6 percent alkaloids in the bark, of which two-thirds is DMT and one-third is N-methyl tryptamine. *Desmanthus illinoensis* is a hardy perennial herb that grows up to three feet tall.

It is native to North America, from North Dakota to Texas, west to Colorado and east to Ohio and Kentucky. These plants grow naturally in small patches scattered throughout the prairie. They also grow well in disturbed soil such as in waste areas, and along roadsides where many patches appear to thrive despite regular mowing. They are often found on rocky, open, or wooded slopes. It contains substantial amounts of DMT and other alkaloids.

Diplopterys cabrerana is a tropical vine that contains high amounts of DMT in its leaves, and lesser amounts in the vine. *Mimosa hostilis* is a drought-resistant shrub that has fernlike leaves and contains DMT in its root bark. It is mostly found in Mexico, and all areas south.

Phalaris grass is a DMT-containing grass that grows in many parts of North America, including many areas in the United States.

MAOIs are regulated by the government, but there is usually no problem buying, possessing, or using them. DMT is a Schedule I drug, and it is closely regulated by the DEA. The plants that contain it are legal to buy, own, and grow, and there are many sites on the Internet that sell them.

The DEA has typically not paid much attention to people purchasing DMT-containing plants like *Psychotria viridis.* There is one case where the DEA did take notice of an unusually large amount of DMT-containing plant material being brought into the United States for use by the UDV religion. In that case, the U.S. Supreme Court ruled that the government cannot control the purchase or use of ayahuasca ingredients by the UDV. The decision was based upon the Religious Freedom Restoration Act of 1993. This law stated that "the framers of the Constitution, recognizing free exercise of religion as an unalienable right, secured its protection in the First Amendment to the Constitution." The law went on to state "governments should not substantially burden religious exercise without compelling justification."

The intent of the law was reportedly to create further protection for religious practice. The law was in response to a U.S. Supreme Court case *Employment Division, Department of Human Resources, Oregon v. Smith,* 1990. In this court decision, it was decided that two individuals who worked as counselors for a drug and alcohol treatment program could not be fired for using peyote. The use of peyote was a sacramental part of the worship of the Native American church they belonged to.

The freedom to use ayahuasca as part of religious observance was upheld in the Supreme Court case *Gonzales v. O Centro Espírita Beneficente União do Vegetal,* 2006. This case involved the 1999 seizure of more than thirty gallons of ayahuasca that was meant for the church. In a unanimous decision, the U.S. Supreme Court ruled that the government could not interfere with ayahuasca being imported for religious purposes.

Custom's action involved a very large amount of ayahuasca, not typical of the amount ordered by most people, and only the religious use of ayahuasca was protected.

An interesting scientific study on ayahuasca was conducted by Erik Hoffman, Jan M. Keppel Hesselink, and Yatra-W. M. da Silveira Barbosa. These researchers examined the effects of ingesting ayahuasca on the electroencephalograms (EEG) of twelve individuals. An EEG measures electrical activity from the brain by placing several electrodes on the scalp. The nerves in the brain communicate by electrical activity. Measuring this electrical activity provides a great amount of information about the brain's functioning. Their study found significant increases in alpha and theta activity from ingesting ayahuasca.

Alpha waves usually occur during states of deep relaxation. High alpha waves are usually associated with feelings of peace, well-being, and low anxiety. Theta waves are unusual in that they are associated with daydreaming, fantasizing, and certain sleep states, as well as periods where one is very focused on a task. Further research is needed to determine whether these EEG states are consistent with the subjective experiences of those using ayahuasca.

Chemistry and Physiological Effects

The essential ingredients for an ayahuasca potion are a plant substance containing MAOI harmala alkaloids and a plant substance containing DMT. These different plant substances may contain other alkaloids that have differing physiological effects. The information regarding the physiological effects and pharmacology of alkaloids other than harmala alkaloids and DMT is limited. However, there is a significant amount of information regarding MAOI harmala alkaloids and DMT.

MAOIs, like the harmala alkaloids, block the activity of naturally occurring enzymes in the body. These enzymes break down chemicals like serotonin, dopamine, and DMT. Because their breakdown is prevented, blood levels of these chemicals increase. This effect of increasing brain chemicals like serotonin is the reason that MAOIs have been used as antidepressants.

The problem with using MAOIs is that they also interfere with the breakdown of foods containing tyramine. Eating foods containing tyramine while taking an MAOI can result in extremely high blood pressure, convulsions, and death. Anyone using an MAOI should avoid foods that contain tyramine for at least a day afterward.

Foods to Avoid

red wine and sherry

caviar

pickled and dried herring

smoked or cured sausages (Italian sausage is okay)

luncheon meats

fava beans

Italian green beens

sauerkraut

snow peapods

tofu

miso soup

cheeses (cream cheese is okay)

yeast (baked bread is okay)

DMT was first synthesized in 1931 and was demonstrated to be hallucinogenic in 1956. It is a white, pungent-smelling, crystalline solid. It is insoluble in water, but soluble in organic solvents and aqueous acids. There is a lack of research on how DMT causes its effects.

The DMT molecule is similar to the neurotransmitter serotonin, and it is likely that it hits several of the same sites as serotonin does. However, more research is needed. Dilated pupils, hypertension (high blood pressure), and increased heart rate are common physiological effects. It has a half-life in the blood of about fifteen minutes.

How People Obtain and Use Ayahuasca

The simplest way that people get the two essential ingredients for ayahuasca is to go to an Internet search engine and type in the ingredient they are looking for (e.g., banisteriopsis caapi, psychotria viridis, syrian rue, acacia madenii, desmanthus illinoensis, diplopterys cabrerana, mimosa hostilis, or phalaris grass). The website eBay is also a place where many people sell fresh and dried ayahuasca ingredients. Here are three companies that have put together premeasured ayahuasca packs with all the ingredients for an ayahuasca potion:

www.azarius.net
www.giftsfromtheancients.com
www.highstreet.nl

Other online companies offering ayahuasca ingredients:

www.ethnobotanicals.com
www.maya-ethnobotanicals.com
www.shamanshop.net

DMT in its pure form is illegal in the United States. However, there are probably hundreds of plants that contain

DMT. The U.S. government has generally not treated DMT-containing plants as illegal, but in a few cases they have tried to stop the importation of DMT-containing plants. Basically, DMT-containing plants can be purchased without a problem, but there is always a risk that the DEA or U.S. Customs will decide that the plants are also illegal.

So what do people do once they have ordered and received their ayahuasca ingredients? Some recipes for making aya-huasca appear below. One general thing to consider when making ayahuasca is that the pH of the water used to boil the ingredients has some effect on the extraction of the alkaloids. Many users recommend always adding a teaspoon of lemon or lime juice to an ayahuasca brew to get a good pH.

The recipes below are for a dose for an average person (what-ever that is). Weight will greatly affect the dosage needed, as will a person's sensitivity to substances. A smaller person who is sensitive to substances might need a smaller dose. A large person with a low sensitivity to substances may need to double the dose.

Ayahuasca Recipe 1

This recipe uses the live (i.e., not dried) versions of *Banisteri-opsis caapi* and *Psychotria viridis* to produce a potion for one person.

Combine 500 grams of fresh *Banisteriopsis caapi* vine and 85 grams of fresh *Psychotria viridis* leaves. Crush the *Banis-teriopsis caapi* and *Psychotria viridis* together and place in a pot. Add enough water to cover. Boil the mixture for four hours. Add water if needed, but make the potion as thick as possible. After the four-hour boil, strain as much liquid as possible from the mixture. Take the remaining solid matter and add some water. Boil for another four hours. After four hours, again strain the liquid out of the mixture and combine with the previously strained liquid. What you have now is ayahuasca for one person. You can drink it or put it into a pot and boil off more of the water in it before you drink it.

Ayahuasca Recipe 2

This recipe uses *Mimosa hostilis* as the DMT ingredient and syrian rue seeds as the MAOI.

Measure 12 grams of dried *Mimosa hostilis* and grind it to a powder. A coffee grinder works well. Next, grind 3 grams of Syrian rue seeds. Place the ingredients in a pot with a teaspoon of lemon or lime juice and enough water to cover. The lemon or lime juice will aid in the extraction of alkaloids. Boil for four hours. Add more water if needed. When done, strain off the liquid using a coffee filter. Drink the potion.

Ayahuasca Recipe 3

This recipe uses dried *Diplopterys cabrerana* as the DMT ingredient and dried *Banisteriopsis caapi* as the MAOI.

Combine 15 grams of dried *Diplopterys cabrerana* with 40 grams of dried *Banisteriopsis caapi* and grind together, possibly with a coffee grinder. Place in a Crock-Pot, along with 1/4 cup of lemon juice. Add enough water to cover and cook for six hours. Add water only if the mixture dries out. Strain every-thing through a coffee filter and collect the liquid. Then add a little water to what is left in the filter and strain again, to rinse out what you want. You can drink the liquid from these two strainings, or put it in a pot and boil off some of the water.

Ayahuasca Recipe 4

This recipe uses dried *Psychotria viridis* as the DMT ingredient and dried *Banisteriopsis caapi* as the MAOI.

Combine 30 grams of dried *Psychotria viridis* with 30 grams of dried *Banisteriopsis caapi* and grind them to a powder, pos-sibly with a coffee grinder. Place them in a pot along with 1/4 cup of lemon juice and enough water to cover the ingredients. Boil for three hours. Add water as needed to prevent it from burning. Filter this through a coffee filter and collect the liq-uid. Return the dry ingredients to a pot and cover them with water. Boil for another three hours, adding water if needed to prevent burning. Filter again with a coffee filter and collect the liquid. Combine this with the previously collected liquid and drink, or boil it down to remove some of the water from it before drinking it.

Other Combinations

Here are a couple of other combinations of MAOI ingredient and DMT ingredient that have been recommended (these would be ground and boiled with your water, lemon juice, etc.).

• 30 grams dried *Banisteriopsis caapi* with 9 grams dried *Mimosa hostilis*
• 5 grams of syrian rue seeds with 30 grams dried *Psychotria viridis*

The Ayahuasca Experience

Most people who use ayahuasca report that they vomit early on in the experience. Vomiting is a side effect of the MAOI. Traditional users view it as an important part of the experience. The body is cleansing itself by purging, which leads to a purification. Regardless, all users report that after vomiting, their nausea subsides, and they then enjoy the experience.

Ayahuasca is a hallucinogen with effects roughly similar to LSD or psilocybin-containing mushrooms. People typically report hallucinations and experiences that involve the jungles, where ayahuasca was originally used, and jungle animals. Some people believe that these images are due to the way ayahuasca affects the brain. Others think that they are just due to the users' expectations of what they will experience. A few descriptions of ayahuasca experiences follow.

Veteran Ayahuasca User Describes His Experience

"Ayahuasca brought up whatever I needed to experience in the present moment. During my ayahuasca session, I entered into a state of intense suffering where I was absolutely convinced that the world would never end, and even death would not release me. Yet those states did pass.

"At another point I found myself spontaneously breathing out love into the world. It was a subtle experience but very distinct. Ayahuasca also helped me to see that a great deal of what I experience is a projection of my mind."

Experienced Stoner's First Ayahuasca Experiment

"I sat on my couch and watched television while awaiting the effects. For ten minutes or so I felt absolutely nothing. Then I decided to stand up and walk. The ayahuasca hit me like a freight train. In one second a massive load of nausea took over my entire body. This was very intense! I felt too inebriated to walk around my house and the nausea was growing more uncomfortable. I decided to sit in my bathroom and await the inevitable purge that I was sure would soon take place. As I walked in and looked in the bathroom mirror I noticed that I had this familiar appearance to myself that I have noticed while experiencing *Salvia divinorum*. After vomiting I felt much better, so I returned to the living room couch.

"Now forty-five minutes had passed since initially consuming the ayahuasca and the trip developed toward a very intense level as I sat on my couch. Thousands of confused thoughts raced through my mind. I felt like I could barely move my body at this point. I had prepared some music prior to the trip but decided at this time that it would be too intense to listen to. Then I reached my hand up to feel my head, and it felt as though my head was disintegrating into millions of particles of universal energy.

"I thought this had to be the peak, but I worried that there could be yet another intense peak soon to come (since it wasn't even an hour into the trip). I stood up and began walking around. I sat back down and after trying to listen to music with my headphones (and finding that it was in fact too intense), I sat and watched TV and tried to help myself come down from the trip.

"I questioned why anyone would ever want to ingest aya-huasca, and I started to think that I should no longer experiment with psychedelics. I also realized that every drug seems to lead to this same headspace but most do not take one very far and many include false senses of euphoria. Ayahuasca was taking me very far on this path to the void, though. My thoughts were a very delicate balancing act between hopeful euphoria and the most dreadful dysphoria I have ever felt. I think that ayahuasca does not make one feel a particular way (such as good or bad); rather, it takes away the meaning for such words and it leaves one struggling to decide on what it is that is being felt under its influence.

"The trip continued in the form of pure utterly over-whelming thought for three more hours. At four hours after ingestion, ayahuasca had let me out of its grips and released me back to reality again. It was another amazing experience. Ayahuasca has taught me things that I couldn't have even have begun to imagine without it as my teacher."

Former Hippie Tries Ayahuasca for the First Time

"The visual effects were astounding. I was not perceiving things through my eyes. I didn't have a body. Closing my eyes did not change the scene in any significant way. There were icons and images of things reminiscent of Inca or perhaps ancient Egyptian religious art. These images were always moving and evolving in some kind of way. There were translucent wormlike things inside my legs, but at the time I didn't realize that they were my legs.

"The hallucinations were in no way similar to LSD hallucinations. These things were real, ever-present, and in perfect clarity. The quality of light had also changed in some way I cannot explain.

"The first hour was indescribably intense. I knew I was insane, and I doubted that I would ever recover. I did not even know what being sane meant. I could not remember what it was like to be normal. During the second hour, I spent more time at the baseline emotion and some time at the euphoric. The euphoria seemed to be because I had "seen it all" and come through relatively unscathed—my mind hadn't been completely unhinged by the experience.

"I was beginning to feel as though my mind was now capable of dealing with the onslaught of this realm of the souls—as if I now belonged there. At one point I wanted to know about my family. The third and fourth hours after ingestion were spent discussing, in what seemed like profound detail, the experience with a friend who was present.

"By the fourth hour, I was back on Earth and not really suffering any effects, although I was extremely shell shocked and still believed everything I experienced to be absolutely real (more real than the rest of my life). Even the next day this feeling remained, and I spent most of my time reliving and trying to deal with my experience."

Some Risks of Using Ayahuasca

The most common complaint of ayahuasca users is that they vomit. The good thing is that the vomiting usually takes place before the peak of the experience. The ayahuasca experience can be intense. Precautions should be taken to ensure a safe environment when taking ayahuasca. All things that one will need during the duration of the experience (e.g., food, water) should be made available ahead of time.

The addiction potential for ayahausca is low. The intensity of the experience is such that it is not something that most people want to do on a daily basis. The need to avoid certain foods while using an MAOI has been previously discussed. Obviously, if a person were to eat one of these foods, he or she would be at risk for serious problems. DMT use produces an increase in heart rate and blood pressure. If someone has a preexisting cardiovascular problem, DMT could cause some difficulties. Aside from this, no other physiological problems with DMT, and ayahuasca use, have been identified.

A theoretical risk of the use of ayahuasca is serotonin syndrome. I say "theoretical risk" because it is something that in theory could happen, but I was unable to find any actual cases of serotonin syndrome caused by ayahuasca.

Serotonin syndrome is caused by excess serotonin in the brain. MAOI interferes with the breakdown of serotonin, just as it interferes with the breakdown of DMT. DMT is a serotonin antagonist, meaning that it interferes with the breakdown of serotonin in the brain. Both MAOIs and DMT increase serotonin in the brain.

The risk of serotonin syndrome increases greatly if an individual is taking a selective serotonin reuptake inhibitor (SSRI). SSRIs are certain medications for depression and anxiety, such as Prozac, Lexapro, Celexa, Luvox, Paxil, and Zoloft. SSRIs slow down the breakdown of serotonin, increasing its levels in the brain.

Symptoms of serotonin syndrome include hypertension, hyperthermia, confusion, hallucinations, agitation, shivering, sweating, fever, muscle twitching, and tremors. In severe cases, serotonin syndrome can be fatal.

CHAPTER 5

GOWIN' NUTS: Betel Nuts

(Areca catechu, Pinang)

Description and History

Betel nuts are the seeds of the betel palm or betel nut tree *(Areca catechu)*. This species of palm produces a medium-size tree that grows to 20 meters tall. Its trunk measures 20 to 30 centimeters in diameter. The leaves are approximately 1.5 to 2 meters long, with numerous, crowded leaflets. It most likely was first cultivated in Southeast Asia. Betel nuts are now grown in India, Vietnam, Malaysia, and Taiwan. Penang Island, located off the west coast of Peninsular Malaysia, is named for the local word for betel nuts, pinang.

Betel nut chewing has been done for thousands of years. Ancient texts refer to its use. Betel nut chewing is cited as one of eight enjoyments, or bhogas, of royal life in the eleventh-century text called Manasollasa. Marco Polo made notes of betel nut use in the late 1200s. An Indian cookbook from about AD 1500 mentions the preparation of betel nut paan. A Persian ambassador named Abdul Razzak visited India and wrote about the effects of betel nut chewing in the fifteenth century.

In Taiwan, drivers can stop at betel nut kiosks to get betel nut chews to keep them awake as they drive on down the road. Competition for business has led to the kiosks using scantily clad women to sell the betel nuts to male drivers. These women have become known as betel nut beauties or betel nut girls. In 2000, Taiwanese director Lin Cheng-Sheng released a movie titled *Ai ni ai wo*. In English, the movie is titled *Betelnut Beauty*, and it features a character who works as a betel nut sales girl.

Betel nuts contain many chemicals, but the primary one responsible for its psychoactive effects is arecoline. In India and parts of Southeast Asia the betel nuts are chewed with mineral lime (calcium oxide), which aids the absorption of arecoline. The lime acts to keep the active ingredient in its freebase or alkaline form, which enables it to enter the bloodstream sublingually.

The chopped nuts and mineral lime are typically rolled in a leaf and then placed in the mouth to be slowly chewed. It has been estimated that betel nut chewing is the fourth most popular habit worldwide, after the use of tobacco, alcohol, and caffeine.

The U.S. DEA does not regulate betel nuts and they are not a scheduled substance. This means that as far as the DEA is concerned, it is legal to possess and use betel nuts. Despite the DEA's lack of betel nut regulation, there are reports that both the U.S. Food and Drug Administration and the U.S. Department of Agriculture have at times seized betel nuts being shipped into the United States. Hence, there may be some advantage to buying betel nuts within the United States.

Chemistry and Physiological Effects

Arecoline is the primary psychoactive substance in betel nuts. It is an alkaloid that is soluble in water, alcohols, and ethers. Arecoline has central nervous system effects similar to those of nicotine, and its chemical structure is similar to that of nicotine. Arecoline is a muscarinic agonist, which constricts the pupils of the eye and the bronchials of the lungs. EEG studies suggest that arecoline affects similar mechanisms in the brain to amphetamines. Rat studies show that it has effects at muscarinic receptors. Arecoline is metabolized mostly through the liver and kidneys. There is a lot of research examining its metabolism. One such study can be accessed online at www .pubmedcentral.nih.gov/articlerender.fcgi?artid=1482804.

How People Obtain and Use Betel Nuts

Betel nuts are, at the time of this writing, legal in the United States. Entering "buy betel nuts" into any Internet search engine will bring up a number of businesses from which to purchase them. A few reputable sources:

www.psychoactiveherbs.com
www.giftsfromtheancients.com
www.iamshaman.com

In addition to the betel nut, edible lime (hydrated calcium oxide) and betel pepper leaves are also needed to make a quid (a small wrap placed in the lip for chewing) that is psychoactive.

Some sources sell betel nut extracts (e.g., psychoactiveherbs) and some sources sell premade betel nut chews (e.g., iamshaman). People who use betel nuts always combine them with the mineral lime to make a chew, or buy a chew with the mineral lime already included. It is expected that an extract will also require the use of mineral lime.

How to Make a Betel Nut Quid/Chew

To make a betel nut quid, use a betel pepper leaf (also sometimes called piper betel leaf or simply betel leaf, about a quarter of a betel nut (you will need to chop the whole nut or you may be able to buy them presliced), and a pinch of edible lime (hydrated calcium oxide). Some people also add a little bit of gambir flavoring, turmeric, cardamom, or catechu gum from the acacia tree. Take one betel pepper leaf and place on top of it 1/4 of a betel nut and the pinch of edible lime. A flavoring like those mentioned above may be added for taste. The leaf is then wrapped around the ingredients to form a quid. This quid is then placed inside the cheek or lower lip and sucked on like chewing tobacco.

The Betel Nut Experience

Betel nuts are a stimulant and their effects are often described as similar to those of nicotine. In addition to its stimulating effects, it is sometimes described as producing a pleasurable or euphoric feeling. Suppression of appetite is also commonly reported.

A Neighbor Tries Some Betel Nuts

"Betel nut has nowhere near the intensity of amphetamines; it is much more like having drunk several cups of coffee. Betel nut is definitely stimulating and mildly euphoric. It is something that I should chew when I need to stay up late and write a paper. I liked it; don't get me wrong. I felt more alert. I felt more able to do what I needed to do."

Random Guy at Beach Tries Betel Nut Quid

"Colors seemed off and it was like everything was bright. I definitely felt stimulated. It was not exactly like caffeine or nicotine, but similar."

Some Risks of Using Betel Nuts

The most common danger of long-term use of betel nut chews is an increased risk of mouth cancer. The International Agency for Research on Cancer (IARC) lists betel nuts as a known carcinogen. Countries where betel nut use is common have much higher rates of oral cancer. Officials at Taipei City's Department of Health reported that betel nut chewers are twenty-eight times more likely to develop mouth cancer than the general population. Ninety percent of those in Taiwan who have mouth cancer were at one time betel nut chewers. Other cancers, such as stomach, liver, prostate, and cervical, are also more common in betel nut users.

Other Risks

• Physical and psychological addiction. The impact of betel nut addiction in Taiwan appears similar to that of tobacco addiction in the United States.

• Betel nut usage during pregnancy may increase the risk of birth defects and spontaneous abortions.

• The CNS-stimulating effects of betel nuts also result in increased blood pressure, with a related increase in risk of stroke and heart attack.

• Research indicates that betel nut use can worsen symptoms of asthma.

• Betel nuts affect blood sugar, which may cause problems for those suffering from diabetes.

• Betel nuts will stain the teeth and gums over time. However, teeth-whitening treatments can be effective in reducing or eliminating the stains.

• The dangers of betel nut use seem to follow a pattern similar to that of using tobacco.

Individuals who use only on rare occasions are unlikely to have negative effects, though they can occur. The risk of negative effects increases with the increased frequency and amount of use.

CHAPTER 6

SMOKING THE PSYCHEDELIC TOAD OF THE SONORAN DESERT:
Bufo alvarius Toad Venom

Description and History

Yes, toad venom! The *Bufo alvarius* toad is native to the Sonoran Desert. The Sonoran Desert occupies 120,000 square miles in southwestern Arizona, southeastern California, most of Baja California, and the western part of Sonora, Mexico. It includes Palm Springs, California, and Phoenix, Arizona.

There are more than 200 species in the genus *Bufo*. All *Bufo* toads have parotid glands on their backs. The parotid glands produce many biologically active compounds, including the neurotransmitters serotonin, epinephrine, and dopamine. All *Bufo* toads are believed to produce a psychoactive chemical called bufotenine.

Bufotenine is a Schedule I controlled substance in the United States. Using bufotenine to alter consciousness is illegal, but owning a toad that makes it is not. The *Bufo alvarius* toad is the only known species that also produces the psychoactive substance 5-methoxy-dimethyltryptamine (5-MeO-DMT), which is not illegal in the United States. *Bufo alvarius* toad venom usually contains a much greater amount of 5-MeO-DMT than bufotenine.

Bufo toads (though probably not of the *alvarius* variety) have been a part of North American human culture for thousands of years. The *Bufo* toad is depicted in the art of the Olmecs, Aztecs, and Mayans. An Olmec burial site in San Lorenzo contained the remains of several *Bufo marinus* toads. Thousands of *Bufo* toads were found in burial vessels in Seibal, Mexico. There are also reports that the Mayans used a drink containing toad venom, called Chicha, as part of their rituals. Curanderos are also reported to have used toad excretions as part of their medicines. Natives in Peru used *Bufo* toad venom on their cuts.

Tales of toad licking began in the 1960s. These were probably more urban myth than reality. Later, when the U.S. Drug Enforcement Agency made bufotenine illegal as a Schedule I substance, stories of people licking toads became common. In actuality, licking a toad would have no mind-altering effect, because the psychoactive chemicals are not active orally. A person could, of course, die from swallowing toad venom, but would not get high.

The amount of 5-MeO-DMT and bufotenine in *Bufo alvarius* toad venom is going to vary, but an average estimate is that dried venom contains about 15 percent 5-MeO-DMT and about 3 percent bufotenine. Any given venom excretion can vary significantly from this.

Chemistry and Physiological Effects

Bufo alvarius venom may contain many things, but the two substances that are most responsible for its effects are 5-MeO-DMT and bufotenine (also called 5-OH-DMT). So this information regarding the chemistry and physiology of *Bufo alvarius* toad venom will be focused on the effects of these two chemicals.

5-MeO-DMT is a short-acting tryptamine that is very similar in nature to dimethyltryptamine (DMT). It is usually found as very small white crystals that appear similar to table salt. Rat studies have shown 5-MeO-DMT to be active at serotonin (5-HT) receptors in the brain, specifically 5-HT1A and 5-HT2.

Bufotenine (5-OH-DMT) is a tryptamine that has similarities to the neurotransmitter serotonin. As with 5-MeO-DMT, it is active at serotonin receptors.

How People Obtain and Use *Bufo alvarius* Toad Venom

I do not know of anyone who sells *Bufo alvarius* toad venom. However, it is possible to buy *Bufo alvarius* toads. The people who wish to smoke *Bufo alvarius* venom must either find a toad or buy one. The easiest method is to purchase the toad. Going on the Internet and typing into an Internet search engine "buy bufo alvarius," will bring up some options. A couple of online sources are at www.bouncingbearbotanicals.com and www.herbalfire.com.

Learning how to catch toads is a task beyond the scope of this book. Several field guides on wild toads and frogs exist, which may be a place to start. One could also contact someone selling the toads and ask for direction.

Once the *Bufo alvarius* toad is obtained, the purchaser can then move on to extracting its venom. The venom is contained in specialized glands. The most obvious and prominent of these is a pair of large kidney-shaped glands located on both sides of the toad's neck. There are also glands located on the outside of the hind legs between the knee and thigh, on the hind legs between the knee and the ankle, and on the top of the front legs. These glands have been described as appearing like warts on the toad.

In order to extract the toad venom, a plate or some other flat object (e.g., a mirror) is needed. Take the toad firmly in one hand and use the thumb and forefinger of the other hand to squeeze at the base of the gland and squirt the venom onto the plate or mirror. This is done for each of the toad's glands. Reportedly, after an hour or two, this procedure can be repeated.

Once the toad has been milked of its venom, it will take four to six weeks before it can be milked again. The venom appears milky in color. The venom is then allowed to dry and obtain the texture of rubber cement. It is then scraped from the plate or mirror.

At that stage the venom is ready to smoke. It can also be stored in an airtight container for later. When the venom is heated, it will liquefy and then start to vaporize. Typical marijuana pipes are not good for smoking the venom, because it turns to liquid. Pipes that can be used for smoking opium work well. Heating the venom and inhaling the vapors through a tube is probably the most common and simplest method.

The amount of 5-MeO-DMT and bufotenine contained in toad venom will vary, which makes it difficult to predict a good psychoactive dose. People typically report smoking between 20 milligrams and 100 milligrams at a time. Some people have reported dosages as high as 200 milligrams.

The *Bufo alvarius* Toad Venom Experience

The effects of smoking *Bufo alvarius* toad venom come on quickly. Users typically describe an intense "rush," which one person described as feeling like having been thrust into another world.

Feeling like one's skin is tingling is often reported at the beginning of the experience. Visual perception is strikingly altered. Things appear distorted. Colors appear more intense, and visual illusions of colors or shapes often occur. The visual experience is most intense with the eyes closed. Perception of sound is altered and actual auditory hallucinations are reported by some. The experience of time is altered, with most people describing a sensation of time slowing down. Some users report feelings of euphoria, but the intensity of the experience can also produce anxiety and panic.

The effects of inhaling *Bufo alvarius* toad venom are similar to other psychedelics, but the effects reach an intense peak rapidly and then quickly subside. Within a few minutes, the experience begins to wind down. The primary experience usually is over in ten to fifteen minutes. Some sense of being mildly altered may continue for up to an hour.

Some Risks of Using *Bufo alvarius* Toad Venom

Smoking of *Bufo alvarius* toad venom can be irritating to the throat and lungs. As with other psychedelics, individuals who are mentally unstable or who have a predisposition for psychosis are at risk for longer-term negative psychological effects. Increases in heart rate and blood pressure can also be problematic for those susceptible to cardiovascular problems. There does not appear to be any problem with physical addiction, though further research is needed to determine this definitively.

CHAPTER 7

TRIPPIN' ON TUSSIN:
Dextromethorphan
(DXM, Robo, DM)

Description and History

Dextromethorphan (DXM) is an over-the-counter cough suppressant available in several brands of cold medicine. In dosages much higher than those used to control a cough, it acts as a dissociative. A dissociative is a substance that results in a feeling of detachment or separation from oneself. Dissociatives differ from hallucinogens and psychedelics, in that hallucinations are not a primary feature. However, some dissociatives can produce mild hallucinations. In addition to DXM, the drugs ketamine and phencyclidine (PCP) are usually considered dissociatives.

DXM was patented in 1954 and it was approved for use by the FDA in 1958. DXM was originally released in the United States as a cough suppressant under the trade name Romilar. It was marketed as a "non-narcotic" cough suppressant to be used as an alternative to codeine. Codeine was being widely used as a cough suppressant, but people were also using it for the euphoria it produced. Codeine also had a potential for addiction, and DXM was seen as a better alternative. There are reports from the beatnik era that the psychoactive effects of DXM were known and that it was used recreationally by some. In 1973, Romilar was removed from store shelves. In the 1970s, DXM became available in the form of cough syrups.

From the 1970s, DXM use became more common, but when access to the Internet became commonplace, the use of DXM became widespread. Information about its psychoactive properties was readily available. The fact that it could be purchased without a prescription in most drug and grocery stores made it especially popular among young people, who were not able to legally buy alcohol. Many adults also engaged in its use, and there are many people who report having gained significant psychological insights as a result of its use (much like those who used psychedelics for enlightenment).

DXM is an unscheduled drug in the United States. This means that it is legal to possess, sell, and ingest. Products containing the substance are regulated by, and must be approved by, the FDA. Despite its federal legality, many states have placed regulations on its sale. Individuals who are interested in purchasing it will have to look up the law in their state. The states that regulate DXM sales typically do things like require that a person be eighteen years old or older. Some states require purchasers to show identification to verify their age. Laws restricting the amount of DXM-containing products one can buy are also common. At the time of this writing, the State of California restricts DXM purchases to three products at a time.

The United States House of Representatives has passed bill H.R. 5280, which makes it illegal to sell DXM in its unfinished active ingredient form. It defines "unfinished active ingredient" as "one of the ingredients in a drug that is not in finished dosage form," or "the sole ingredient of a drug that is not in finished dosage form." In other words, it is illegal to sell pure DXM. The law does allow for the continued sale of DXM as part of a prepared medication, like cough syrup.

At the time of this writing, the bill is waiting to go before the United States Senate for a vote. If the bill passes, it should not interfere with being able to buy DXM cough syrup or tablets in the drug or grocery store. The purpose of the legislation appears to be to try to stop the online sale of pure DXM. This action was prompted by cases in which individuals purchased pure DXM over the Internet and subsequently overdosed. It seems that people are less likely to overdose if they have to swallow massive amounts of cough syrup, as compared to being able to easily ingest large amounts of the pure form.

In 2005, two teenagers died from an overdose of pure DXM that they ordered over the Internet from Indiana. The story of the deaths of these two teenagers was spread widely in the media, along with a few other apparent DXM-overdose-related deaths. It was likely the publicity surrounding these cases that has led to the focus on making pure DXM illegal.

Preparations containing DXM typically come in pill or syrup (liquid) form. Many products containing DXM also contain other substances used for the treatment of cold and flu symptoms. The substances include acetaminophen (Ty-

lenol), guaifenesin, pseudoephedrine, aspirin, chlorpheniramine maleate, and others.

Some of these other substances, when taken in the high
doses that a DXM user takes, can cause serious health problems or even death. High doses of acetaminophen can cause
severe liver damage. Pseudoephedrine is a stimulant that increases heart rate and blood pressure. This stimulant effect
presents dangers for those at risk for strokes or other cardiovascular problems.

The Internet has a wealth of information about the DXM
experience. One website, "The Dextroverse," can be found at
www.dextroverse.org. It is described as "a dxm community."
The site lists all kinds of information about the psychoactive
use of DXM, and one can also communicate with others who
are interested in the substance.

In addition to the cough suppressing and psychoactive effects of DXM, research is being done on using high doses of
DXM to treat certain medical conditions. One of these conditions is peripheral neuropathy, a condition in which the peripheral nerves are damaged, causing substantial numbness
and pain. DXM appears to help reduce the pain from peripheral neuropathy by acting at N-methyl d-aspartate (NMDA)
receptor sites. Dosages to treat peripheral neuropathy pain are
in the range of 300 to 400 milligrams per day. It has also been
used with some success to treat fibromyalgia.

The problem with using DXM to treat these illnesses is that
the dosage that reduces pain also tends to result in psychoactive effects. For this reason, DXM may not be practical as a
pain treatment.

Chemistry and Physiological Effects

DXM's status as a legal drug has allowed for a lot of research into how it works and how it is metabolized in the body. Its chemical structure has similarities to the opiate narcotics, though it is not an opiate. In its pure form it appears as white crystals. It is minimally soluble in water and freely soluble in alcohol.

When taken orally, DXM is absorbed from the gastrointestinal tract. It then enters the bloodstream and crosses the blood-brain barrier. DXM is metabolized by the hepatic system into dextrorphan, the 3-hydroxy derivative of DXM. The psychoactive effect of DXM is believed to be caused by both the drug and this metabolite. DXM is also metabolized by liver enzymes to produce other metabolites, which may or may not be involved in its psychoactive effects.

DXM binds to multiple sites in the brain. It has a high affinity for Sigma 1 and PCP2 sites, and lesser affinity for other brain sites. The metabolite dextrorphan is much more potent than DXM at the NMDA receptor. The NMDA receptor is the central site of dissociative action, and it is probably the main contributor to most of DXM's effects. Dissociatives act on the NMDA receptor by binding to its channel once it opens up, essentially plugging it up. It is this NMDA blockade which is probably responsible for the visual flanging (i.e., a phenomenon of sensory perception in which sensory data seems to be split up into obvious "frames") experienced by many DXM users. Memory problems resulting from DXM use are also likely due to this NMDA blockade.

How People Obtain and Use Dextromethorphan

DXM can be purchased at most drug and grocery stores. A would-be user has to be aware of state laws that might control the sale of DXM-containing substances. For example, one can buy three DXM-containing products at a time in California.

The major concern for individuals who buy DXM for the purpose of ingesting and altering their consciousness is to make sure that what they buy contains only DXM and no other "active ingredients" that can make them sick. All cough and cold medications, whether tablets or syrups, list their active ingredients on the bottle. The only active ingredient should be dextromethorphan. It is technically dextromethorphan hydrobromide (HBr), so dextromethorphan, dextromethorphan hydrobromide, and dextromethorphan HBr are all the same thing. Safeway's Maximum Strength Tussin Cough is one source. Robitussin Maximum Strength Cough is another source. There are many other brand and generic sources available. People who use DXM check the list of active ingredients on the cough suppressant product they use to make sure that it only contains DXM, and not some of the other common additives to such products (e.g., acetaminophen, guaifenesin, pseudoephedrine, aspirin, chlorpheniramine maleate).

The dosage of cough syrup or tablets that one takes for the psychoactive effects is much greater than what one would take to quiet a cough. DXM-containing cough syrup typically comes in four-ounce, eight-ounce, and sometimes twelve-ounce bottles. A typical dose of a DXM-only cough syrup (meaning that it has no other active ingredients besides DXM) is four to eight ounces. People who do it a lot and who have developed some tolerance may do as much as twelve ounces.

A four-ounce bottle of Safeway Maximum Strength Tussin Cough contains 354 milligrams of DXM. Thus a typical psychoactive dose of DXM is between 350 and 700 milligrams, with heavy users using 1,050 milligrams. The recommended therapeutic dose for controlling a cough is 30 milligrams every six to eight hours. As was discussed earlier, one can take enough DXM to overdose. Estimates of the amount of DXM that would lead to death cover a wide range, from approximately as low as 2,300 milligrams to as high as 20,000 milligrams.

The Dextromethorphan Experience

DXM is classified as a dissociative. The dissociative experience has similarities to that of hallucinogens, but with the dissociatives, hallucinations are absent or minimal. A predominant part of the DXM experience is a feeling of dissociation or disconnection from one's normal self. The individual typically feels as if he is somehow sitting back and observing himself. The dissociative substances have been described as interfering with the transmission of signals from other parts of the brain, especially sensory signals, to the conscious mind.

This decrease in the normal inputs into consciousness can allow a user to engage in self-exploration without the normal mental garbage that interferes with introspection. It can also lead to feelings of panic and anxiety due to the feeling that one has lost oneself. Differentiating one's internal experience from what is happening external to oneself often becomes difficult, leading to confusion as to what is real and what is imagined. This can result in paranoia for some, especially when there is a lot of external stimulation.

The majority of people report the experience as pleasant or even euphoric. Other individuals have experienced intense anxiety, panic, and paranoia. The negative mental effects are more common as the dose increases.

Visual perception is altered, as is the ability to keep things in visual memory. Closing the eyes produces intense visual effects. The ability to visualize things in one's mind, while the eyes are closed, increases. The perception of time is often altered, with users reporting time slowing down. Speech can become altered and more difficult. At higher doses, one may have difficulty forming words. Physical effects often include increased sweating, nausea, and sometimes vomiting. Increased heart rate is often reported.

In addition to the mental dissociation experienced, a sense of feeling less in touch with one's body is often reported. The typical strain one feels when lifting something heavy is absent or decreased. People often report feeling stronger, but this may just be due to the decreased sensation of strain on one's muscles. This lack of connection with one's physical body can also interfere with coordination and balance.

Recovering Cocaine Addict and Psychotherapist Tries DXM

"I am writing this a couple of days after it happened. This has been a life-changing experience for me. DXM is unlike other substances I have taken. When under the influence of other substances, I have often felt like I had some great insight or knowledge about the world, but once the high was over, the insights seemed to fade away. What made sense to me when I was under the influence seemed ridiculous upon becoming sober. This was totally different with DXM. What I learned from my DXM experience stayed with me until today. I feel changed.

"They call DXM a dissociative. It made me feel like I left myself. I was able to step back from who I was and take a look at myself without any of the encumbrances that usually interfere with me being able to take an honest self-exam. With DXM I did dissociate. I stepped back and looked at who I was. I evaluated myself without any bias. I then was able to think about the person I would like to be. What is more spectacular is that I was able to then create for myself the experience of myself being the person who I want to be. I experienced what it would be like to be the me I want to be. And like I said before, this sense of how to be who I want to be stayed with me. As I said this was life changing."

UCLA Student Tries DXM for the First Time

"The following is after taking two four-ounce bottles of Tussin. It really hit me when I was sitting on the toilet in my bathroom listening to my television. I found myself interacting with the television. It was as if what was happening on the television was happening for real. This lasted for several seconds before I realized that it was just the TV and not reality. I returned to my room and attempted to watch television. Again and again I would lose myself into the television. This lasted for probably an hour or two.

"I then began to turn inward. I began thinking about my life. As I started to get tired, I closed my eyes and I was amazed by the visual hallucinations. With my eyes open I did not hallucinate, but with them closed, I could move through whole worlds."

Thirty Something Woman Tries DXM with Her Boyfriend

"Wow! I was glad that it was just my boyfriend and me. I felt like I had lost myself, so I relied on him to keep me safe. I kept seeing things in my mind. It was a trip. I don't know how to explain it. It was a unique experience."

Some Risks of Using Dextromethorphan

The legality of DXM has allowed a lot of research on the substance. Unlike many other psychoactive agents, DXM has been the subject of a large body of research literature.

There is the possibility of overdose with DXM (as there is with many drugs). Most overdoses have been the result of taking pure DXM. Taking DXM in cough syrup form makes it less likely to overdose because one would have problems keeping down enough cough syrup to do so. That is not to say that overdose cannot occur with cough syrup. It is not possible to say exactly what the lethal dose of DXM is. Obviously, the less one weighs, the smaller the lethal dose would be. As stated above, the typical psychoactive dose is 350 to 700 milligrams, with the lethal dose typically being 2,300 milligrams or more.

Another risk of DXM use, which has also been previously

discussed, is taking a DXM preparation that contains something besides DXM (e.g., acetaminophen, pseudoephedrine). As mentioned, acetaminophen can damage the liver in high doses and pseudoephedrine can increase the risk of stroke and heart attack.

DXM should not be taken by those who are on monoamine oxidase inhibitors (MAOIs). MAOIs are an old class of drugs that are used to treat depression. They are infrequently used as a treatment for depression these days, because they have a lot of side effects and they are not as effective as more recent antidepressants.

The most commonly reported side effect of DXM use is nausea. Other side effects include dizziness, sweating, and erectile dysfunction. These occur when someone is under the influence, and go away after it wears off. DXM is not highly addictive, but there are many cases of people who developed a psychological addiction to the substance.

One issue with DXM that has received a lot of discussion is whether or not using a high dose of the substance multiple times could result in a form of brain damage called Olney's lesions. In 1989, John Olney conducted tests in which high doses of an experimental dissociative called Dizocilpine was injected into rats. Dizocilpine, like the dissociative DXM, produces its effects at least in part by its action as a NMDA receptor antagonist. The rats' brains were subsequently examined and found to have tiny holes (lesions) in the posterior cingulate cortex and retrosplenial cortex regions of the brain. This naturally sparked concern that usage of high doses of DXM could result in similar brain damage.

However, in 2003 researcher Cliff Anderson wrote an article demonstrating that Olney's tests did not provide direct evidence that lesions would develop in the brains of humans following use of dissociatives. Part of Anderson's argument is based on studies of monkeys, whose brains are much more similar to humans than are those of mice. Another researcher named Roland Auer injected monkeys with the dissociative Dizocilpine (the same chemical used by Olney in his rat studies) and it did not cause any lesions. Other researchers have echoed the conclusions of Auer, that dissociatives are unlikely to produce lesions in the brains of monkeys, and similarly, they are unlikely to present a risk of brain lesions in humans.

So what is one to make of these conflicting research results? Well, for one, more research is needed. Until further studies are done, it is not possible to say for sure whether DXM and other dissociatives can cause brain lesions. The majority of evidence at this point supports the view that DXM probably does not produce brain lesions, but this cannot be proven.

CHAPTER 8

THE INTOXICATING PEPPER: Kava
(*Piper methysticum,* Kava-Kava, Kawa, Awa, Waka, Lawena, Sakau, Yagona)

Description and History

Kava *(Piper methysticum)* is a member of the pepper family. It is a perennial shrub that grows up to nine feet tall. Its leaves are bright green and heart shaped. It produces some small flower spikes. Kava is native to the South Pacific islands. The roots of the plant have traditionally been used to produce an intoxicating beverage. The first European documentation of kava use occurred when Captain James Cook took his second trip to the Hawaiian Islands (also called the Sandwich Islands) in the 1770s.

The roots of the kava plant contain a number of non-nitrogenous compounds, which are typically referred to as kavalactones (or kavapyrones). The first compound to be isolated was methysticin in the 1800s. Several other compounds have since been isolated from the plant, including dihydrokawain, dihydromethysticin, desmethoxyyangonin, kawain, and yangonin.

Kava use has been common in the Hawaiian Islands, Tonga, Fiji, Samoa, the New Hebrides, and many islands of Melanesia. In modern times, kava and kava extracts have been available in most drug stores in the United States, where it has been sold as a health supplement. Concern over possible liver damage from long-term heavy use of kava has resulted in many stores discontinuing its sale.

Historically, kava has been used simply for its inebriating effects, which are similar to that of alcohol, but it has also been used for ceremonial purposes. The use of kava is prominent in the mythology of the Pacific islands. There is a Pacific island folktale that tells how kava came to be a domesticated plant. According to the story, a long time ago people drank a drink made from wild kava, but they did not plant kava themselves. One day, two young women were out cleaning yams when a kava plant sprouted and grew into one of the women's vagina. This caused her significant pleasure.

Thinking that this must be some very special kava plant, they took a sprout of the plant and brought it home to plant in their garden. Some years later, the women made a kava drink from the now mature plant and shared it with the men in their village. The men were impressed with the kava, and following further investigation involving a virgin female and such, declared it to be the "true kava." All cultivated kava is said to come from this special strain.

Some pharmaceutical companies have investigated kava for medical use, due to its muscle relaxant and tranquilizing properties, but this research has not resulted in the production of any useful medications. Kava has been shown in several studies to be an effective treatment for anxiety. Research has demonstrated that kava taken orally can reduce pain. It can also be held in the mouth to numb tooth or mouth pain. Kava has been used for weight loss. It is not known if kava has any direct effect upon appetite, but its common side effect of stomach upset makes one less likely to want to eat.

Kava is not a scheduled drug by the United States DEA. It is legal to buy, possess, and ingest in the United States. Despite its legality, some stores have stopped selling it, apparently over concerns that it can be harmful to the liver (more on this below). It is legal in most countries, though some regulate or control it.

Chemistry and Physiological Effects

The onset of the effects from ingesting kava is typically twenty-five to thirty minutes, with the effects lasting from two to several hours. The half-life of the kavalactones is about nine hours. Common physiological effects include muscle relaxation, slight numbing of the lips and tongue, and sedation. Gastrointestinal disturbances and nausea are not uncommon.

Metabolism of kava and its metabolites occurs through renal and fecal excretion. The effects of kava are caused by the kavalactones, of which fifteen have been identified. The exact mechanism of action for the kavalactones still needs to be investigated. It does not appear to effect GABA or benzodiazepine receptors. There is some evidence that kava is a dopamine antagonist. It does not appear to cause physical dependence.

Because kava is a central nervous system (CNS) depressant, it potentiates the effects of other CNS depressants, like alcohol and benzodiazepines.

How People Obtain and Use Kava

The kavalactones are responsible for the psychoactive effects of kava. Of the fifteen kavalactones that have been identified, only six occur in large amounts:

methysticin
dihydrokawain
dihydromethysticin
desmethoxyyangonin
kawain
yangonin

Pure kava root and kava extracts are both available for purchase. Pure kava root contains an average of 15 percent kavalactones, but samples can range from 3 percent to 20 percent. Kava extracts typically range from 30 percent to 70 percent kavalactones. Though the individual kavalactones have some variation in their effects and psychoactive dosages, kava extracts on the market report only the total percentage of them combined and not how much of each individual kavalactone is in the total.

Studies have shown that dosages of 250 mg to 400 mg kavalactones (usually taken three times per day) have anxiety-reducing effects. Intoxicating dosages are typically around ten times that amount, in the range of 2,000 mg to 4,000 mg of kavalactones. When using an extract, it is easy to determine the milligrams of kavalactones contained in a dosage. For example, a 300-milligram capsule of kava extract that contains 30 percent kavalactones will contain roughly 100 mg of kavalactones.

Pure kava root (typically ground) and kava extracts can be purchased at health food stores or on the Internet. Typing "buy kava" into an Internet search engine will produce a long list of sources. Here are a few:

www.kavaking.com (Kava King's phone number is 888-670-5282, extension 29)
www.giftsfromtheancients.com
www.iamshaman.com
www.herbspro.com (Herbs Pro's phone number is 866-915-5300)

Kava extracts are sold in powder form (for mixing with something like juice), in capsules, pastes, liquigels, tinctures, and mixed with things like chocolate. Whatever form one purchases the milligrams of kavalactones determine the intensity of its effects. I Am Shaman (www.iamshaman.com) even sells "Kava Kava Kits" that contain "all the ingredients that make up a 2-person serving of our favorite Kava Kava recipe."

Growing Kava

Some individuals, who have the patience for it, grow kava themselves. A detailed guide to growing kava from the Secretariat of the Pacific Community in Fiji is available online at www.spc.int/cis/PacificKavaProducersGuide/Chap1.html. Kava plants are grown from cuttings. Live plants can be found online by typing "live kava plant" into an Internet search engine. One source of live kava plants online is www.nakamal athome.com.

Kava grows best in shade or partial sunlight. It needs a loose, fertile soil. Kava needs soil that drains easily. The soil should be kept damp, but not wet. The plants are typically harvested in their fourth year, but plants can be harvested as early as eighteen months.

The Kava Experience

At doses below those usually used to produce intoxication, kava typically produces some relaxation and a pleasant feeling. This happens at the typical dose recommended when one follows the direction found on the package of kava sold as a dietary supplement. Many people use it simply for the mildly relaxing effects, without taking the higher doses resulting in intoxication. It is frequently used at small doses to treat anxiety and insomnia.

At larger, intoxicating doses it has effects that are similar to, but not exactly the same as, that of drinking alcohol. One of the first noticeable effects upon ingesting kava is that it numbs the mouth, tongue, and to some degree, the lips. Kava has a bitter, earthy taste, making it difficult to ingest. Some people experience nausea and even vomiting. Within twenty to thirty minutes, feelings of relaxation, contentment, and peace usually occur.

Kava acts directly as a skeletal muscle relaxant. People tend to be more talkative, social, and to feel some heightening of senses. Unlike alcohol intoxication, a moderately intoxicating dose of kava does not seem to impair and blunt the senses. At larger doses, the experience becomes more like that of alcohol drunkenness. Larger doses usually result in significant sedation and sleep. The primary part of the experience lasts approximately two to three hours, with a mild lingering effect up to eight hours.

College Student Tries Kava for the Second Time

"The first thing I noticed was the numbing of my lips and tongue. It tastes gross. Then the calming, euphoric effect came on. I felt drunk, not exactly like on alcohol, because I was still in control of most of my faculties. There was definitely a euphoric effect. Other parts of my body seemed to be numb. This lasted for a couple of hours, followed by a need to sleep."

Thirty Something Social Worker Drinks Kava

"Within minutes my entire mouth was numb. I began to experience very relaxing thoughts. I had a peaceful outlook. I had the ability to make sense of things, to put things into perspective. I was surprised that something legal could have this strong of an effect. I felt content and happy to be where I was. It was very relaxing."

Some Risks of Using Kava

The biggest concern with kava use is the question of whether it might cause damage to the liver. There are some anecdotal reports of long-term, heavy kava users who develop symptoms similar to jaundice, including yellowing of the eyes and skin.

Kava became a focus of the U.S. Food and Drug Administration (FDA) after a number of European reports that it might cause damage to the liver were published. German and Swiss health authorities identified approximately thirty such cases, including four cases requiring transplantation, and one death. In the United States, the FDA had received several reports of kava-related liver damage, including a report of a previously healthy young woman who required a liver transplant.

Because of these reports, a group of U.S. trade associations hired a professional toxicologist to evaluate the potential relationship between kava consumption and liver problems. His report concluded that, based on the lack of specific clinical and historical information, "there is no clear evidence that the liver damage reported in the U.S. and Europe was caused by the consumption of kava." More research is needed to determine the effects of kava on the liver. The majority of evidence seems to indicate that occasional use of kava is unlikely to have any negative effects upon one's liver, but the possibility of liver damage from chronic usage still needs to be examined. Concern has also been expressed that kava's negative effects upon the liver may be increased with heavy alcohol usage because alcohol is damaging to the liver.

Long-term users also often develop dry, scaly patches of skin. This dry skin goes away when they stop using kava. The exact cause of the dry skin is unknown, but it may relate to kava interfering with cholesterol metabolism.

CHAPTER 9

OPIUM'S KISSING COUSIN: Kratom
(Mitragyna speciosa, Ketum, Ithang, Thom)

Description and History

Kratom *(Mitragyna speciosa)* is a leafy tree that grows in Thailand and other parts of Southeast Asia. It grows to about fifty feet tall and fifteen feet wide. It has yellow flowers and dark green leaves. Kratom is an evergreen, meaning that it has leaves all year round. Kratom trees grow best in wet, fertile soil. They are drought- and frost-sensitive. The trees are also likely to fall victim to some types of fungus.

The first written report of kratom use was by H. Ridley in 1897. By the time of his report, kratom use was common throughout Southeast Asia, suggesting that it had been used for a long time there. Ridley's work focused upon kratom as a treatment for heroin addicts. Kratom hits most or all of the same sites in the brain that heroin does. This means that it will minimize, or even prevent, heroin withdrawals. Some studies have looked at kratom as an alternative to methadone for treating heroin addicts. These studies show that kratom is probably superior for treating heroin addicts. However, there have only been a couple of studies done and more research is needed before kratom will be accepted as a replacement for methadone.

In 1907, E. Holmes published an article about using kratom as a substitute for opium. Also in 1907, D. J. Hooper isolated the main psychoactive alkaloid of kratom. This alkaloid was again isolated in 1921 by E. J. Field, and he named it mitragynine. By 1940, three alkaloids in addition to mitragynine were identified. Ultimately, twenty-five alkaloids would be identified in *Mitragyna speciosa*. The most abundant alkaloid is mitragynine, with smaller amounts of speciogynine, paynanthine, speciociliatine.

The international kratom trade experienced a serious threat in the first few years of the twenty-first century, when a large amount of bogus kratom entered the marketplace. It appears that most of this material originated from an individual named Bruno Philips of Ebotashop, located in France. Phillips and his helpers marketed the product to a number of retail sellers of ethnobotanicals, apparently with some success. Phillips made an error in trying to sell the material to Daniel Siebert, a *Salvia divinorum* expert and advocate. Siebert noted that the leaves Phillips was selling did not resemble kratom leaves. Subsequent scientific analysis of the material verified that it was not kratom, and that it did not contain the alkaloid mitragynine.

An article by Jon Hanna in the Vernal Equinox, 2003 edition, of *The Entheogen Review* reported that at least a hundred kilograms of the bogus material had been sold by Phillips. It seems unlikely that the sale of the fake kratom was a mistake by Phillips, because even once he was informed of the nature of what he was selling, he continued to try to sell it to the uninformed. At the time of the writing of this book, it appears that Phillips and his bogus kratom have gone away, but this incident reminded many people of that old saying, "buyer beware."

The mitragynine molecule has some structural similarities to yohimbe alkaloids. Chemically, mitragynine is 9-methoxy-corynantheidine. It is soluble in alcohol, chloroform, and acetic acid. The alkaloid content of *Mitragyna speciosa* (kratom) is about 0.5 percent, of which about half is mitragynine. The average weight of a fresh leaf of *Mitragyna speciosa* is approximately 1.7 grams, and the average weight of a dried leaf is approximately 0.43 grams. This should give you some idea of how much mitragynine and other alkaloids are in each leaf. I have been told that about twenty leaves of *Mitragyna speciosa* should contain about 17 mg of mitragynine.

Recent research on kratom indicates that another molecule 7-hydroxymitragynine (7-OHM) also contributes to kratom's psychoactive effects. This research also indicates that 7-OHM may contribute more to kratom's psychoactive effect than does mitragynine.

People in Thailand identify two different types of kratom. The two types are differentiated by the color of the veins in the leaf. One type of kratom leaf has mostly red veins and the other type has mostly green/white veins. There is no scientific research regarding the differences between the two. Some anecdotal reports say that there are no differences in the mental or physical effects of the two types. Other anecdotal reports claim the green/white-veined variety is a little more potent, but that the red-veined variety produces an experience of being more alert while still relaxed.

In Thailand, most kratom use is done by chewing the fresh leaves. People in Thailand also use the leaves in cooking or to make tea. The Thai people generally view kratom users as better than opiate users. Kratom has some stimulant effects, which may make users work harder than they would without it. The Thai government passed the Kratom Act 2468, which went into effect on August 3, 1943. This law made it illegal to ingest kratom, and it also required that kratom trees be cut down and no new trees planted. It made possession of one ounce of kratom extract a capital offense.

Kratom is not controlled by the U.S. government. It is legal to buy, possess, and cultivate. If it is sold for human consumption, it would fall under regulation by the FDA. For this reason, most kratom is sold with the statement "not for human consumption."

Chemistry and Physiological Effects

As stated above, kratom contains many alkaloids. Studies of the chemistry and physiological effects of kratom have focused on two molecules that have been identified as contributing to its psychoactive effects. These two molecules are mitragynine and 7-OHM. There is little or no information regarding the pharmacology and physiological effects of the other alkaloids in kratom. Therefore, the information on the pharmacology and physiological effects of kratom is based on studies of these two molecules. Mitragynine and 7-OHM both have effects

similar to opiates. They are both cough suppressant and analgesic. They attach to most of the same receptor sites in the
brain that opiates attach to. Kratom suppresses opiate withdrawal and its effects are reversed by opiate antagonists such
as naloxone.

Pure mitragynine is a white, amorphous powder with a
melting point of 102–106°C and a boiling point (bp5) of 230–
240°C. Mitragynine binds to alpha-adrenergic receptors. Mitragynine produces a reduction in smooth muscle tone, local
anesthesia, and central nervous system depression. It decreases
2-deoxy-D-glucose-stimulated gastric acid secretion. 7-OHM
is thirty to forty-six times more potent than mitragynine and
seventeen times more potent than morphine by weight. Its
potency is the reason that recent researchers think it is the
primary cause of kratom's psychoactive properties. 7-OHM
interacts with all three major opiate sites, delta (5.6%), kappa
(4.6%), and mu (89.8%). There is a lack of information regarding the metabolism of kratom. Specifics of how kratom is
removed from the body will need to be researched.

How People Obtain and Use Kratom

Traditionally, kratom was used by chewing the leaves of the
tree. Extracts from the leaves are now available and provide
a much more potent way to use kratom. Most people report
that your best bet for getting the kratom experience is to buy
an extract. Going to a search engine like Google, and entering
"kratom extract" as a search will bring up a list of many sellers. Here are several good sources of kratom extract:

www.psychoactiveherbs.com
www.ethnobotanicals.com
www.giftsfromtheancients.com
www.iamshaman.com

The website eBay is also a resource for kratom extract. The amount of active ingredients in samples of kratom extracts varies. For this reason, people typically do a little experimenting to determine their ideal dosage.

I have received firsthand reports of people using a sample of kratom extract from www.psychoactiveherbs.com to determine the psychoactive amount. They tried the 15 powdered extract. One teaspoon was definitely psychoactive. Some of them wanted more, so they took up to three teaspoons of extract. This seemed like plenty for a maximum dose.

Kratom extracts are typically combined with some sort of liquid so they can be drunk. Juices, such as orange juice, pineapple juice, apple juice, and cranberry juice, are typically used as mixers. The literature on kratom typically states that kratom does not produce nausea; however, some people have found kratom extracts nauseating. Others swear that kratom extracts are not upsetting to the stomach at all. One way to reduce the likelihood of nausea is to place the extract into gel capsules. Typing "gel capsules" into any Internet search engine (e.g., Google) will bring up many sources for them. Following are a couple of resources for gel capsules:

www.capsuline.com
www.capsuleking.com

www.capsugel.com
www.good-earth.com/herbs-empty-gel-capsules.html

The Kratom Experience

Kratom is different from opiates in that a low dose is more stimulating to the human body than depressing. People in Thailand that chew on the kratom leaves, as opposed to using the extracts that have recently become available, get a low dose of the active chemicals. For this reason, people in Thailand typically view kratom users as much more active and successful than opiate users. When dosages of kratom increase, as is possible with the currently available extracts, the effects are more similar to those of opiates. Opiate users typically describe its effects as similar to a high dose of codeine. These users say that it does not produce the intense high of shooting heroin.

As with the opiates, kratom users find that physical and emotional pain is reduced. Itching and sweating are common. People often report an increased appreciation for music. The effects typically last between two and six hours, depending on the dose and the weight of the individual.

An experiment reported in the Vernal Equinox, 2004, edition of *The Entheogen Review,* by Altoid, described the experiences of ten individuals who used kratom. Of the ten people who tried kratom, eight reported having a positive experience and two reported having a negative experience. The negative effects experienced by the two individuals were nausea and vertigo. Two of the subjects who reported having a positive experience were heroin addicts who wanted to get off the drug. These two individuals used kratom while quitting heroin to decrease their withdrawal symptoms. Both reported that kratom significantly decreased their withdrawal symptoms and allowed them to sleep on the first night of being heroin free. This decrease in withdrawal symptoms made it much easier for them to quit heroin.

Neuropathy Sufferer Tries Kratom

"It took about forty-five minutes to come upon me. I started to feel really happy. The pain in my body was gone. No pain. I felt like no anxiety. This state of contentment—bliss—lasted for a little over an hour. Then I started to feel tired. An overwhelming need to lay down. Not necessarily to sleep, but to do nothing . . ."

Philosophical Musician Tries Kratom

"Initially I felt comforted. I felt an inner sedation and contentment. Then the feeling of needing to vomit and purge came, but it felt like a positive purging. Like I was removing the toxins from my body. I then returned to the couch and rested. Toward the end I felt really shut down. Like I can't move, shut down. My breathing started to slow, like it was going to stop. . . . it was definitely an interesting physical experience. I would do it again just for that."

Correctional Officer on Leave Describes Kratom Experience

"There was a strong sense of pain reduction. I had actually used it for back pain before, and it worked better than any reasonable dose of a pharmaceutical. The desire to work was enhanced, but my vision and thinking processes were altered as if intoxicated. The euphoria was extremely intense, and it felt very real and clean. I feel like I'm trying to hide something or used them as some sort of escape, but this seemed to actually help me through things. I got some empathy and heart-opening happiness that caused me to talk about personal issues. Unlike other opiates/opioids, I didn't feel like it was for nothing the next day. There was somewhat of an opiate hangover, though I didn't crave and feel the detox. I felt satisfied. It is without a doubt my favorite opiate-like drug."

A Friend Gives Kratom a Try

"My vision was extremely distorted, and there was actually a mild hallucinogenic effect. The trees seemed to sway a bit, and my sense of vision was enhanced. Colors seemed brighter, and the euphoria was beyond powerful. I was really warm."

Some Risks of Using Kratom

The biggest risk of using kratom is probably that it is habit forming. Addiction has become such a problem in Thailand that using it has been made illegal. However, occasional use of kratom will not likely lead to addiction. Daily users of kratom typically develop extreme weight loss, dark pigmentation of the face, erectile dysfunction, and withdrawal symptoms if they quit using. Withdrawal symptoms include muscle aches, irritablity, runny nose, diarrhea, and muscle jerks. There is no definitive information available regarding the dosages of Kratom that would result in a death by overdose. In searching the Internet for overdose cases, none could be found. Kratom is a CNS depressant, like heroin, and as with heroin, it is expected that overdose is possible. Further research is needed on the risks of kratom use.

CHAPTER 10

THE ACID ALTERNATIVE:
Morning Glory and Hawaiian Baby Woodrose Seeds
(Heavenly Blue, Pearly Gates, Flying Saucers, Ololiuhqui)

Description and History

The morning glory *(Ipomoea violacea)* plant and the Hawaiian baby woodrose *(Argyreia nervosa)* plant are two distinct species. They are being covered together here because their seeds contain the same psychoactive ingredient and they are used the same way. Despite the similarities, the amount of the psychoactive chemical present in their seeds differs, resulting in differences in the amount of seeds typically consumed for their psychoactive effects. The psychoactive chemical they contain is called ergine, d-lysergic acid amide, LSA, and LA-III. All four of these names refer to the same chemical. To make things simple, this writer will refer to it by the abbreviation LSA.

The differing names for LSA have to do with the history of its discovery. LSA was labeled ergine when it was discovered to be a chemical produced by ergot, a fungus that infects the grain rye. Ergot poisonings were common during the Middle

Ages when people would eat rye that had been infected with this fungus. Poisoning by ergot would often cause individuals to convulse about (or dance), foam at the mouth, "speak in tongues," and experience hallucinations. This bizarre behavior, or "dancing mania," was labeled "Saint Vitus' Dance." In the seventeenth century it was discovered that alkaloids produced by ergot were the cause of "Saint Vitus' Dance," and this understanding brought about a great decrease in ergot poisonings.

Midwives have used ergot as part of their work since the Middle Ages. It was recognized that the chemicals produced by ergot could produce uterine spasms, and thereby childbirth could be induced. The uterine-constricting properties of ergot alkaloids led to research in the 1930s by Albert Hoffman at the Sandoz laboratories. Hoffman began synthesizing chemicals from ergot for use in obstetrics. His work eventually led to the creation of the compound d-lysergic acid diethylamide on November 16, 1938. He gave this chemical the code-name LSD-25. This is the LSD that would become the popular drug "acid" of the 1960s and beyond. The substance LSA is structurally very similar to LSD. It has psychoactive effects that are similar to those of LSD, though it has a lower potency.

The first written accounts of the use of morning glory seeds come from Spanish writers in the sixteenth and seventeenth centuries. They reported the use of the seeds by the Aztecs and other groups in Mexico. They referred to the seeds as "ololiuhqui" seeds, which means "round things." They reported that they came from a plant called coaxihuitl or coatlxoxouhqui. Natives in Mexico used these seeds as part of their shamanic rituals and as part of shamanic medicine.

In the 1930s, Blas Pablo Reko sent a sample of the seeds to C. G. Santesson in Sweden. Santesson reported that the seeds were psychoactive, but he did not identify the chemical that caused their psychoactive properties. In 1960, Albert Hoffman, the discoverer of LSD, isolated and identified LSA as the psychoactive chemical in morning glory seeds. The seed samples had been sent to Hoffman by R. Gordon Wasson, who was in Mexico researching the use of psychedelic mushrooms by the native people there.

Morning glory seeds are legal to buy and possess in the United States. The psychoactive chemical in them (LSA) is a Schedule III controlled substance. Being a Schedule III drug means that it has a legitimate medical use (I don't know what that is, but it sounds good), and that its abuse potential is less than that of Schedule I and Schedule II drugs. This writer is not aware of any cases in which the government has gone after someone for use of morning glory or Hawaiian baby woodrose seeds, though the fact that they contain LSA does not rule out such a possibility.

There are several varieties of morning glory, but the *Ipomoea violacea* type is the one most commonly used for its psychoactive properties. Common varieties of *Ipomoea violacea* that are used for their psychoactive properties are heavenly blue, pearly gates, flying saucers, and wedding bells. Heavenly blue is the earliest cultivated of these varieties. Occasional white mutations of the heavenly blue variety occurred, and one of these mutations was used to develop the pearly gates variety. The pearly gates variety was released to the public in 1942. Darold Decker released the flying saucer variety in 1960. This variety was developed from mutations of the pearly gates variety. Decker also developed the wedding bells variety, which was released in 1962.

As natural products, morning glory seeds will contain varying amounts of LSA. Hawaiian baby woodrose seeds also contain LSA, but in concentrations about two to three times the amount that morning glory seeds do. LSA has somewhere between one-tenth to one-thirtieth the potency of LSD.

Chemistry and Physiological Effects

The psychoactive chemical in morning glory and Hawaiian baby woodrose seeds is d-lysergic acid amide (LSA). LSA is active at serotonin receptor sites in the brain (5-HT2A and 5-HT1A). It is primarily metabolized by the liver and excreted by the kidneys. There is a need for further research regarding its physiological effects.

How People Obtain and Use Morning Glory and Hawaiian Baby Woodrose Seeds

Many morning glory seeds that are available in stores have been treated with chemicals that can make you vomit if you ingest them. Most people who use the seeds for their psychoactive properties buy them online for this reason. Going to an online seller of seeds, it is usually pretty obvious if they are selling the seeds for the purpose of ingesting them. Putting "buy morning glory seeds," or "buy Hawaiian baby woodrose seeds" into most Internet search engines will bring up many sources, including:

www.giftsfromtheancients.com
www.iamshaman.com
www.psychoactiveherbs.com
www.bouncingbearbotanicals.com
(Most people use Hawaiian baby woodrose seeds, as opposed
to morning glory seeds, due to their higher potency.)

The typical dose of Hawaiian baby woodrose seeds is between six and twelve seeds. The seeds are usually ground in a
coffee grinder. The ground seeds are then added to something
like juice or ice cream, and then swallowed. If using morning
glory seeds, at least three times the amount of Hawaiian baby
woodrose seeds (eighteen to thirty-six, or more) is needed.

The Morning Glory and Hawaiian Baby Woodrose Seed Experience

The active chemical of these seeds (LSA) is closely related to
LSD. It makes perfect sense that the effects are typically described as similar to that of LSD, but less intense. Nausea, gas,
and even vomiting are sometimes reported due to the irritating effects of ingesting the ground seeds. Mood is usually elevated in a positive way. Some people experience anxiety or
paranoia because of the mind-altering effects, but this is less
common than that reported with LSD, probably due to the
decreased intensity of the experience.

Alterations in visual perceptions are a typical part of the experience. Lights often cause halo effects, rainbows, and other
visual distortions. Closing one's eyes also results in increased visual experiences. People become more engaged in things around

them. Feelings of deep insight are common. Everything seems more important, and simple things seem deep. Alterations in time perception are frequently reported. Many people report life-changing experiences resulting from using morning glory and/or Hawaiian baby woodrose seeds. Despite the positive effects, some find the mind-altering part of the experience unpleasant.

The onset of effects is usually within twenty to forty minutes. The amount of food one has in the stomach will alter the onset of effect. Some people recommend fasting twelve hours before use to reduce the likelihood of vomiting. Other individuals feel that having some food in the stomach reduces the nauseating effects. The experience peaks at three to four hours. The total duration of effect is five to eight hours.

Former Sixties Hippie Tries Hawaiian Baby Woodrose Seeds

[After taking eleven Hawaiian baby woodrose seeds]

"I have tried LSD twice before and I was expecting a similar, but less intense experience. That was pretty much what I got. It was also a more pleasant experience. I think it is better than LSD. Some things I experienced:

- Watching television and seeing the lights come out from the sides like daggers or swords.
- Sound is not altered like my LSD experiences.
- Lights kept coming at me from the TV."

Some Risks of Using Morning Glory and Hawaiian Baby Woodrose Seeds

There is a lack of research into the possible risks of LSA. Obviously, someone who is under the influence of such a drug could engage in dangerous behaviors. Users of LSD (which is similar to LSA) have on some occasions had psychotic experiences (e.g., hallucinations, delusions) following its use. This writer has not been able to find any reports of psychosis following LSA use, but based upon the LSD experiences, it may be possible. The potential for addiction, as with most psychedelics, is low.

CHAPTER 11

LAUGHING GAS:
Nitrous Oxide
(Laughing Gas, Dinitrogen Oxide, Dinitrogen Monoxide)

Description and History

Nitrous oxide is simply a gas made up of two atoms of nitrogen and one atom of oxygen. It was first isolated by an English chemist and Presbyterian minister named Joseph Priestly (good name for a minister, don't you think?) in 1772. Priestly was not aware of its psychoactive properties.

In 1800, Humphrey Davy, at the Pneumatic Medical Institution in Bristol, reported that the gas had anesthetic properties. Davy said that pain from his toothache was taken away after inhaling nitrous oxide. Davy gave the gas to visitors at the institution. Based on their reactions, he came up with the term "laughing gas."

For the rest of the 1800s, nitrous oxide was often given to audiences during public demonstrations. Probably the most famous public nitrous oxide demonstrator was Gardner Quincy Colton. Colton had spent two years in medical school, but he dropped out in 1844 before receiving his degree. He then traveled around providing demonstrations of nitrous oxide and other scientific discoveries.

On December 10, 1844, a dentist named Horace Wells and his wife attended one of Colton's laughing gas shows. At the show, subjects were given nitrous oxide. They then walked around onstage while under the influence. During the event, one of the participants hit his leg against a wooden settee. The participant reported that he did not experience any pain, apparently due to the effects of the gas. Wells realized that the gas had potential for use in the dentistry field. He asked Colton to come to his office and administer the gas to him (Wells) while he had a tooth pulled. While under the influence of nitrous oxide, his tooth was pulled without pain. Wells had made the discovery of anesthesia.

During the next month, Wells would use nitrous oxide as an anesthesia to extract the teeth of more than a dozen patients. In 1845, Wells and a physician named William T. G. Morton arranged for Wells to give a lecture at Massachusetts General Hospital. During the lecture, Wells was to perform a tooth extraction on a student volunteer. Physicians and students were both present for the operation. During the extraction, the nitrous oxide bag was removed too soon. The patient reported that he felt some pain during the procedure, though the pain was less than it would be without the gas. Because of the report of pain, the general opinion of the group was that nitrous oxide was not impressive as an anesthetic.

However, this demonstration launched investigations into the use of gases for the purpose of anesthesia. Well's colleague and former apprentice, William Morton, started using ether as an anesthetic during dental procedures. Morton shared information about his use of ether with the Massachusetts General Hospital administration and with other physicians. Thus began the modern use of anesthesia in medicine.

Nitrous oxide continued to be used in dentistry. An advance came when it was combined with air and provided to the dental patient during procedures. This method of delivery allowed the patient to receive the nitrous oxide for a prolonged period of time. Subsequently, it was combined with pure oxygen and provided to dental patients.

In modern times, nitrous oxide has become a common part of dentistry practice. Currently, many dentists use nitrous oxide, combined with oxygen, while doing certain procedures. It is used mostly for its anxiety-reducing properties, with its analgesic effects also being of benefit. Despite its wide use in dentistry, there are few, if any, reports of negative effects.

The well-known psychologist and philosopher William James inhaled nitrous oxide and wrote about his experiences in 1889, in an article titled "Consciousness under Nitrous Oxide," in the *Psychological Review*. He also discussed his experience with nitrous oxide in his probably best known work, *The Varieties of Religious Experience*. In that book, he states, "I myself made some observations on . . . nitrous oxide intoxication, and reported them in print. One conclusion was forced upon my mind at that time, and my impression of its truth has ever since remained unshaken. It is that our normal waking consciousness, rational consciousness as we call it, is but one special type of consciousness, whilst all about it, parted from it by the filmiest of screens, there lie potential forms of consciousness entirely different."

The current use of nitrous oxide as a psychoactive substance has a lot to do with whipped cream. Nitrous oxide is used to dispense whipped cream. Many states have passed laws making it illegal to inhale nitrous oxide to get high. Still, because nitrous oxide is legal to use to dispense whipped cream, a lot of it is available. Of course, many companies that sell nitrous supposedly to make whipped cream know they are really selling it for people to get high, but by marketing it for use with whipped cream, they cover themselves legally. Similarly, some purchasers pretend to buy it to enhance their desserts.

In addition to nitrous oxide's use as a psychoactive and an anesthetic, it has other uses. Nitrous oxide injected into a car engine can greatly increase its horsepower. This effect has led many a driver desiring a fast car to have a nitrous oxide setup installed in their vehicle. When you heat nitrous oxide, it breaks down into oxygen and nitrogen. This means that the injection of nitrous oxide into an engine makes more oxygen available during combustion. The presence of more oxygen means you can also inject more fuel, which allows an engine to produce more power. Nitrous oxide is one of the simplest ways to provide a significant horsepower boost to any engine.

Nitrous oxide also improves performance because when it vaporizes, it provides a cooling effect on the intake air. By reducing the intake air temperature, the air's density is increased, which provides more air in the cylinder. The main problem with using nitrous oxide to fuel a car engine is that it is fairly bulky, and the engine needs a lot of it. As with any gas, it takes up lots of space even when compressed into a liquid. For this reason, most cars that use nitrous have only a few minutes' supply.

Some recent research has discovered another promising use

for nitrous oxide. Dr. Jesse Haven, at Anchor Health Center in Naples, Florida, and Dr. Allen Kuhn, at Discover Wellness Clinic, in St. Petersburg, Florida, have investigated the use of nitrous oxide in treating addiction to smoking cigarettes. Their research consists of a small number of case studies, but their results have been promising. The researchers report that one of the bases for the treatment is that smokers who can remain free from cigarettes for just three to seven days have a relatively high likelihood of staying off of cigarettes long term. Previous research has shown that smokers who quit for one week are five times more likely to quit smoking at a six-month follow-up, than are smokers that quit for a day. One-fourth of smokers who quit smoking for a month will be able to abstain from smoking at the one-year point. The use of nitrous oxide seems to help a smoker to get through the crucial early days of abstinence. Nitrous oxide seems to counteract some of the negative effects of nicotine withdrawal.

In their study, subjects were treated with one to two twenty-minute administrations of nitrous oxide during the first three days of quitting smoking. Their treatment resulted in an 85 percent reduction in the number of cigarettes smoked (per day) in the three days following the treatment. Almost all patients reported a decrease in craving cigarettes after the treatment. Most subjects that continued smoking reported a reduction in the number of cigarettes smoked during the few days after the treatment. Larger scale studies are needed, but given the safety of properly administered nitrous oxide, it appears to be a likely beneficial treatment for cigarette addiction.

Aside from the psychoactive use of nitrous oxide, there are concerns about its potential to damage the environment as a greenhouse gas. Some reports say that nitrous oxide can have 296 times the effect of carbon dioxide upon global warming. Nitrous oxide attacks ozone in the stratosphere, potentially increasing the amount of ultraviolet light hitting Earth's surface. Of course, the use of nitrous oxide to get high does not result in large amounts of nitrous oxide being released into the atmosphere. Bacteria in the oceans and ground produce nitrous oxide. Agricultural practices (e.g., the use of nitrogen fertilizers) produce a large amount of the gas. Industrial activity, such as the production of nylon, also contributes some to the nitrous oxide in the atmosphere.

Chemistry and Physiological Effects

Nitrous oxide is a weak anesthetic, and it also produces significant analgesia (pain reduction). Nitrous oxide's use in dentistry and medicine over the past 150 years has allowed time for thousands of studies to be done on the substance. Doing a Medline Search, which is a commonly used resource to search for medical studies, resulted in a list of 14,648 articles. Volumes could be written about all of the research into the gas. This writer will provide just an overview of the chemistry and physiological effects of nitrous oxide. Readers are encouraged to avail themselves of the large amount of other information available online and elsewhere.

Nitrous oxide is an odorless and colorless gas that has been described as having a slight sweet taste. It has a molecular weight of 44. It is stable and inert at room temperature. It is not flammable at room temperature, but can become flammable if raised to a very high temperature. It quickly reaches equilibrium in the blood, and it remains at a constant concentration as long as the gas is consistently administered.

Despite all of the research on nitrous oxide, its exact mechanism of action is still not completely clear. There are some theories about how it may work. Some research has provided evidence that nitrous oxide is active at opioid receptor sites in the brain, and that it produces its effects in a way similar to those of opiates like heroin or morphine. Other research has found that nitrous oxide has no effect at opioid sites. Those researchers who support the theory that nitrous oxide is active at opioid sites have argued that there were problems with the methodology of the research that showed that the gas does not act at opioid sites.

Some research shows that nitrous oxide may have its effects by being a NMDA antagonist. Substances that block NMDA activity typically reduce pain, a finding that is consistent with the effects of the gas. There is also evidence that nitrous oxide has at least a small effect on α-amino-3-hydroxy-5-methyl-isoxazole-4-propionic acid (AMPA) and gamma-aminobutyric acid (GABA) receptor sites.

Nitrous oxide increases blood flow to the brain and it increases pressure in the brain. The gas reduces responses to pain stimulation in the brain stem, but it does not irritate the respiratory tract. Some of its pain reduction may be the result of direct effects on the spine.

How People Obtain and Use Nitrous Oxide

Nitrous oxide is typically sold to the public as a propellant for whipped cream. Whipped cream cans and dispensers for

Magic Mushrooms: *Amanita muscaria* mushroom patch. (Photo courtesy Krystle Cole and www.NeuroSoup.com)

Magic Mushrooms: Dried *Amanita muscaria* mushrooms.

Dried *Artemisia* absinthe/wormwood.

Traditional method of serving absinthe, with water poured over a sugar cube.

Green Fairy absinthe.

Dried *Psychotria viridis* leaves, ayahuasca ingredient.

Dried and shredded *Banisteriopsis caapi* vine, ayahuasca ingredient.

Betel Nut Beauties working at a roadside kiosk in Taiwan.
(Photo by Tobie Openshaw)

Betel Nut Beauty, making betel nut quids. (Photo by Tobie Openshaw)

Betel Nut Beauty, selling betel nut quids to drivers. (Photo by Tobie Openshaw)

Betel Nut Beauty, in nurse outfit. (Photo by Tobie Openshaw)

Dharma, the *Bufo alvarius* toad.
(Photo courtesy Krystle Cole and
www.NeuroSoup.com)

Bufo alavarius toad with glands circled.
(Photo courtesy Krystle Cole and
www.NeuroSoup.com)

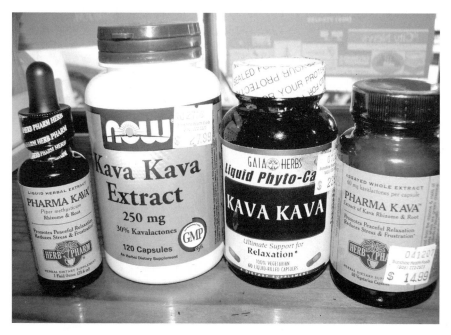

Some available forms of kava, including capsules, extracts, and liquid.

Salvia divinorum 20x extract.

Collection of pipes used for smoking *Salvia divinorum* and other herbs.

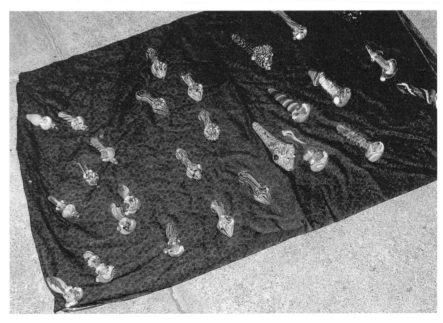

Some artistic glass pipes for sale on a San Francisco street.

Hawaiian baby woodrose seeds.

Coffee grinder with Hawaiian baby woodrose seeds about to be ground. A coffee grinder makes it easy to finely grind all kinds of seeds and dried plant material.

Box of canisters containing nitrous oxide, commonly called "whip-its."

Implements for using nitrous oxide—"cracker" (in two pieces, left and right), nitrous oxide canister, and balloon. Notice that the cracker has a small spike at the bottom to puncture the canister and a hole for the gas to escape into the balloon.

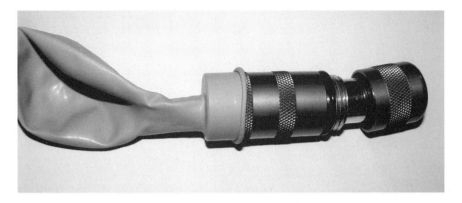

Cracker with nitrous oxide canister inserted and balloon attached, ready to be used.

Balloon filled with nitrous oxide.

Whole nutmegs.

Ground nutmeg.

"Chasing the dragon" method of smoking opium and other substances (e.g., *Bufo alvarius* toad venom) by inhaling the vapors from the heated material. The substance is placed on a piece of tin foil, heated from below with a lighter, and the vapors are inhaled through a straw.

Blue opium poppy seeds purchased from the local grocery store.

Persian white opium poppy seeds purchased online.

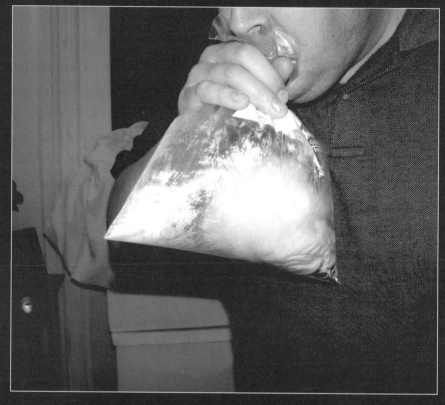

"Huffing" method of inhaling dangerous volatile solvents and aerosols. A rag is soaked in the chemicals, then placed in a plastic bag. The individual inhales the harmful chemicals from the bag to get high.

whipped cream use nitrous oxide to aerate their product. As previously reported, many who sell nitrous oxide realize that most people who buy their product are not using it to whip cream. They need to maintain that façade in order to keep their sale of the gas legal. Following are the two ways that most people obtain nitrous oxide to get high:

Obtaining Nitrous Oxide, Method 1

This method is the least cost-effective way to obtain nitrous oxide, but it is a method that some people use. One can go into any grocery store and buy a few cans of whipped cream. In order to dispense whipped cream from a can, one must turn the can upside-down and press the valve at the top to the side. If one places the can upright and places one's mouth over the top of the valve and then presses it to the side, only the gas in the can will be released. The person then breathes in the gas and holds it in his or her lungs for as long as possible. The individual then takes a breath of air before repeating the process. After a few inhalations the gas will be gone and only some liquid cream will come out.

Obtaining Nitrous Oxide, Method 2

The method that most people use, which is more cost effective, is to buy canisters of nitrous oxide (often referred to as "Whip-Its"). These canisters (also called bulbs) are designed to be used in whipped cream dispensers. They resemble a carbon dioxide canister that is used in BB guns, but they are smaller. The canisters can be bought at many head shops, and they can sometimes be bought at liquor stores. (This writer has a liquor store a few blocks away that sells boxes of them.)

Many people also buy them on the Internet. Typing "buy nitrous oxide" into an Internet search engine will usually bring up many sources for nitrous oxide canisters, including:

www.bestwhip.com
www.nitrousoxidechargers.com
www.legithit.com
www.easywhip.com

Once the nitrous oxide cartridges arrive, the next step is to figure out how to get the gas out of the cartridge. People typically use one of two methods. One method is to use a device, commonly called a "cracker," that punctures the cartridge while a balloon is attached to it to catch the gas. Years ago, this was the most common method of using nitrous oxide. Some head shops (you know, those smoke shops with the odd pipes) still sell them.

More recently, nitrous oxide canisters seem to have become the preferred method. The canisters can also be used for dispensing whipped cream with nitrous oxide, which might be part of the reason they have become the preferred method of use. Sources for canisters to discharge cartridges of the gas can be found by typing "buy nitrous oxide dispensers" into an Internet search engine. Here are several sources for nitrous oxide dispensers: www.whipeez.com

www.creamright.com
www.bestwhip.com

The dispensers usually come with instructions; the user would ignore the instruction to place the cream into the dispenser. Most dispensers look similar to a thermos with a couple of things attached to it. The top usually screws off so that whipping cream can be poured inside. (Of course, the nitrous oxide user would not put the cream in.) There is then an attachment that the nitrous oxide canister can be placed into. This usually screws into the dispenser to puncture the cartridge and release the gas into the dispenser. Some kind of handle or button is then used to dispense the whipped cream. If no cream is in the dispenser, only nitrous oxide is dispensed. Most people dispense the nitrous into a balloon attached to the end the whipped cream would come out of. This is because the gas can be freezing cold when it converts from the liquid in the canister to the gas that is released. The gas can also come out with a lot of force. The person then breathes nitrous from the balloon and holds it in the lungs as long as possible. Then a breath of air is taken before inhaling more nitrous oxide.

The Nitrous Oxide Experience

Inhaling nitrous oxide results in a rapid onset of effects. Most people report a very pleasant feeling or euphoria. Many people break out into laughing, resulting in its reputation as laughing gas. Sounds become more intense and seem to "throb." The body becomes numb, because nitrous oxide is an anesthetic. Users often feel introspective, like they are having a mild psychedelic experience. The periods of introspections do not usually last after the effects of the gas. Many people have reported an increase in sexual arousal, leading some to use the gas as part of their sexual experience.

Young Graduate Student Tries Nitrous Oxide for Fun

[After taking one large inhalation of nitrous]

"I was sitting in a room with a few of my friends. My friend S. put two Whip-Its into a balloon and passed it to me. I had never tried nitrous before. The music playing began to throb in my ears. Feelings of calm. My head became fuzzy. My ears started ringing. Beyond that it is kind of hard to explain. The whole thing faded fairly quickly and I was left with a little headache."

The Same Student Tries Nitrous Oxide Again

[Using a whole box of Whip-Its with a friend]

"The high left so quickly that I found myself jonesing for more right away. I was bummed when we ran out. I remember thinking I had some brilliant insight into life, but I can't exactly recall what it was. Nitrous is like that. You feel like you are having this insightful experience, but it doesn't last. I also remember telling my friend that he could ask me any question and I would answer honestly. It felt like a truth serum. My inhibitions to letting out a secret were gone. I also wondered what it would be like to inhale nitrous during orgasm. Hmm?"

Graduate Student's Friend Has First Nitrous Oxide Experience

"I sucked two puffs from the balloon. A numbness came over my body. My friend sat across from me and burst into laughter. That made me laugh, but not with the same intensity (he had a balloon of his own). The sounds around me became choppy. Things around me moved in and out. It seemed like things were moving in slow motion. I sucked the last bit of nitrous in. Things gradually began to return to normal. The sound chopped slower. Time returned to normal."

Some Risks of Using Nitrous Oxide

The biggest risk of nitrous use is if one does not also breathe air while breathing nitrous. The media occasionally report stories of people who create a situation where they only breathe nitrous oxide and no oxygen and then they die. There are situations where someone has put a bag of nitrous over their head and died. There are also situations where someone has filled an enclosed space with nitrous oxide and died because no oxygen could get in.

When nitrous oxide is dispensed from its liquid form to its gaseous form, it is very cold. For this reason, people usually dispense the gas into a balloon to let it warm. Taking nitrous directly from a canister or dispenser can freeze the lips, throat, fingers, and so forth.

Data indicate that frequent use (like using it every day for many days) leads to a deficiency in the vitamin B12. B12 deficiency results in numbness, tingling, and muscle spasms in the extremities. Long-term B12 deficiency can lead to a host of problems. People should not use nitrous oxide every day. Addicts that cannot control their use should take a vitamin B12 supplement (or even better, take all of the B vitamins).

Aside from the above issues, some people report headaches after using nitrous oxide. Drowsiness after using the gas is also sometimes reported. Less common, but also reported, is nausea.

CHAPTER 12

THE PSYCHEDELIC IN GRANDMA'S PANTRY: Nutmeg

(Myristica fragrans, Mace, Rou dou kou, Indian nut)

Description and History

The nutmegs are a group of evergreen trees belonging to the genus *Myristica*. There are several trees in this genus, including *Myristica argentea, Myristica inutilis, Myristica malabarica,* and *Myristica otoba,* but the nutmeg of interest here is *Myristica fragrans. Myristica fragrans* produces the seed most of us know as the spice nutmeg. People sprinkle this ingredient on their eggnog and add to certain baked goods, puddings, sausages, and pies for a little zing. It is also the one nutmeg that is psychoactive when ingested. It can be purchased ground or whole in almost all grocery stores.

Nutmeg trees are native to Indonesia. The tree grows to an average height of thirty feet. It has numerous branches and has been described as resembling an orange tree. The leaves are bright green and glossy on the top and a dull greenish-white on the bottom. The fruit resembles a small peach. The nutmeg seed has an outer covering that starts out fleshy, but becomes dry and leathery later. The outer covering turns yellow when ripe. The red part of the outer covering of the nutmeg seed, called aril, is used to produce the spice mace. Mace is described as similar in flavor to nutmeg, but less sweet.

The nutmeg seed is about two centimeters wide and four centimeters long. It is brown in color. Despite its name, it is not actually a nut. Trees grown from the nutmeg seed take about eight to nine years to flower and bear fruit. Once mature, the trees can continue to bear fruit for many centuries.

One of the earliest documents describing nutmeg use was written by the Roman writer and philosopher Pliny in the first century AD. Pliny described a tree called comacum that produced a fragrant nut and a perfume of two kinds. He was probably describing nutmeg. There is evidence Arabs and Indians were using nutmeg as a medicine long before the birth of Christ. During the sixth century AD, nutmeg was brought to Europe by Arab traders. Crusaders returning from the Middle East may have also brought the spice back with them, and it was well known throughout Europe by the Middle Ages.

Portuguese explorers discovered the islands where nutmeg was grown in the 1500s, and for a period of time they had a monopoly on its trade. The Dutch subsequently took over the islands, along with control of the nutmeg trade, in about 1621. The Dutch were accused of burning plantations of nutmeg trees to keep the supply low in order to keep prices high. The high price of the seed resulted in its being associated with wealth. It was seen as a delicacy of the rich, and high-priced eateries would allow diners to grate their own nutmeg at the table.

Though the Dutch controlled most of the nutmeg trade,

the British were involved in the trade on a small level. In the late 1700s, the British took over the nutmeg-growing islands ruled by the Dutch and then gained a monopoly on its trade. The British established nutmeg plantations on many of their other conquered islands, resulting in the West Indies becoming a major supplier of nutmeg. Grenada is second only to Indonesia in the production of nutmeg. Grenada's flag features a yellow and red nutmeg pod on the left side, indicating its importance to the island.

The historic trade in nutmeg was for its use as a spice. It is not known when its psychoactive properties were first discovered. The earliest documentation of its psychoactive effects is from the 1500s, when a pregnant woman became delirious after ingesting several nutmegs. Her use of nutmeg was likely the result of a false belief that ingesting large amounts of nutmeg could result in the abortion of an unwanted fetus. In the 1800s and early 1900s, the reputation of nutmeg as being able to induce abortion had become widespread. This belief likely resulted in many women becoming aware of the seed's inebriating properties.

In addition to its ineffective use to end pregnancy, it has been recommended throughout much of the world to treat a range of ailments. It has been mentioned in western medical books as a treatment for liver damage, stomach problems, the plague, scarlet fever, insomnia, and bad breath. It was also an herb used in traditional medicine in Southeast Asia. Throughout Asia, as well as England, nutmeg was prescribed as a treatment for rheumatism. It continues to be used in Indian and Arabic folk medicine in modern times.

Nutmeg has been used as an aphrodisiac in parts of the

Middle East. In India it was sometimes added to food to increase sexual desire. Modern research conducted in India has added support to this traditional use of nutmeg. Studies published in the journal *BMC Complementary and Alternative Medicine,* in 2003, volume 3:6, and 2005, volume 5:16, examined the effect of nutmeg on the sexual behavior of male rats. Male rats administered nutmeg did show an increase in sexual activity. In addition to their increased horniness, they also had erections for longer periods, and they were able to repeat sex after a shorter latency period (i.e., perform sex again shortly after ejaculating). They did not study females, but perhaps this research will be of some help to those women with a male partner who needs some assistance. Further research is needed to determine whether these results apply to human males. The traditional use of nutmeg suggests that it may also increase human sex drive, but we will have to wait for definitive evidence.

The literature contains occasional mentions of nutmeg's inebriating effects following the above-mentioned case from the 1500s. However, it was not until the 1900s that reports of its use for its mind-altering properties became more widespread. It was in the U.S. prison system where the use of the herb as a drug became a common occurrence. Nutmeg was popular in the prisons because it was legal and could be easily obtained from the prison's kitchen. The controlled prison environment also resulted in drugs like marijuana and heroin being available inconsistently, often making nutmeg the only psychoactive substance to be found.

In Malcolm X's autobiography, he described being introduced to the intoxicating effects of nutmeg while incarcerated. He reported that at least a hundred other inmates were using it. Inmates would pay their fellow inmates who worked in the kitchen with money or cigarettes for matchboxes full of stolen nutmeg. The drug experimentation that began with the 1960s resulted in the use of nutmeg expanding beyond the prison walls.

Nutmeg is roughly 50 percent cellulose or solid matter and 50 percent oils. Of these oils, about 20 percent are called volatile oils. The rest are called fixed oils. The volatile oils contain the chemicals most likely responsible for the psychoactive effects of nutmeg. These chemicals, which make up only a small portion of the chemicals contained in the oils, are myristicin, elemicin, and safrole.

- *Myristicin,* technically known as 4-methoxy-6-(2-propenyl)-1,3-benzodioxole, is a colorless oil. It is insoluble in water, but soluble in ether and benzene. It has a boiling point of 173°C. It makes up about 4 percent to 8 percent of the volatile oils, and approximately 1 percent of the total weight of nutmeg. Studies in humans and nonhuman animals have supported the psychoactive effects of myristicin. Myristicin is common in other plants, including carrots, celery, parsley, and black pepper.
- *Elemicin,* technically known as 3,4,5-trimethoxy-1-(2-propenyl)benzene, is chemically similar to myristicin. It has a boiling point of 175°C.
- *Safrole,* technically known as 5-(2-propenyl)-1,3-benzodioxole, is a slightly yellow oil. It is insoluble in water, but soluble in ether and chloroform. It has a boiling point of 232 to 234°C. The FDA classifies safrole as a carcinogen, though some researchers disagree. Safrole was once a common ingredient in root beer, but due to its suspected carcinogenic activity the FDA banned its use as a food additive. It was also banned for use in soap and perfumes. An interesting fact about safrole is that it is often used as a precursor to

MDMA (3,4-methylenedioxy-N-methylamphetamine), most commonly known as ecstasy, E, X, or XTC. Many sites on the Internet describe how to convert safrole to MDMA. The budding chemist should be aware that the DEA pays close attention to purchasers of safrole.

The DEA has been long aware of the psychoactive effects of nutmeg and its use as a recreational drug. Despite this, nutmeg continues to be legal to sell, purchase, possess, and ingest throughout the United States. Nutmeg is not currently a controlled substance. Nutmeg's popular use as a spice, its relatively low risk of serious negative health effects, and its low risk of addiction have probably resulted in the DEA not taking any action to limit nutmeg use.

Chemistry and Physiological Effects

Information about how the chemicals myristicin, elemicin, and safrole cause their effects is limited. In 1967, Alexander Shulgin published a chapter in the book *Ethnopharmacologic Search for Psychoactive Drugs* (editor, D. H. Efron), in which he proposed that the effects of these three compounds were the result of their being metabolized into other known psychoactive compounds, including MDMA (ecstasy). The fact that the chemical safrole can be converted in a lab to MDMA lends support to Shulgin's theory. However, subsequent research on rats has been unable to confirm it.

Research has demonstrated that myristicin is active at serotonin receptors in the brain. Physiologically it acts as a depressant. It decreases blood pressure, and it has sedative and anesthetic properties. It has also been demonstrated as being hallucinogenic and antidepressant. Elemicin is also active at serotonin receptors in the brain, where it has anti-serotonergic properties. Like myristicin, it decreases blood pressure, produces hallucinations, and acts as an antidepressant.

Little information exists regarding the physiological effects of safrole. Like myristicin and elemicin, it is likely that it is active at serotonin receptors.

How People Obtain and Use Nutmeg

Nutmeg is available ground or whole in any grocery store. No studies have examined whether nutmeg loses any of its psychoactive properties once ground, but some people report that freshly ground is more potent than pre-ground. If bought whole, the spice can be ground in a coffee grinder. It may be necessary to break it into pieces using a knife or hammer to prevent it from just bouncing around in the grinder.

The amount of the psychoactive chemicals present in nutmeg varies significantly. The variations must be taken into account when one uses it for its psychoactive properties. Recommended dosages range from two teaspoons to a high of five teaspoons. Most people find ingesting nutmeg unpleasant. Nutmeg is typically mixed with something else to make it more palatable. Acidic juices, like orange juice, help cover up its taste. Mixing melted chocolate, chocolate syrup, ice cream, and sherbet with nutmeg has also been recommended.

The Nutmeg Experience

Ingesting nutmeg typically takes two to three hours to cause an effect. If one's stomach is empty, the effect may come on earlier. If one's stomach is full, the effect may take four to six hours. Due to the length of time it takes for the effects to start, many people report thinking they did not take enough or that they have been misinformed about the effects.

The initial effects are described as similar to a mild marijuana or alcohol buzz. Cotton mouth and bloodshot eyes are common at this early stage. Users often feel lightheaded and senses seem enhanced. Many people report nausea and even vomiting, though this is not experienced by all. Time seems slowed, everything seems funny, speech becomes slurred, coordination is impaired, and closing the eyes results in something similar to visual hallucinations.

The experience typically peaks at around the seventh to ninth hour, and it lasts for about three hours. Speech becomes more slurred and coordination resembles that of someone drunk on alcohol. Auditory hallucinations are common, as are closed-eye visual hallucinations. The high then subsides. During the next ten to fifteen hours, users describe feeling worn out, weak, sleepy, relaxed, and hung-over. It is commonly reported that even though feeling very tired and exhausted, the user cannot fall asleep.

Some people report that the overall experience is enjoyable, worthwhile, and that they would try it again. Many others report that the experience is quite unpleasant. Those who report a negative experience often complain of the nausea, severe exhaustion while not being able to sleep, prolonged and unpleasant hangover, paranoia, and other negative mental effects. Whether due to negative effects, the length and intensity of the experience, or something else, nutmeg use has never gained widespread popularity. Addiction appears highly unlikely, and even those who report enjoying the experience do not repeat it frequently.

Thirty-something Friend Describes His Nutmeg Experience

"I started with one tablespoon as a reasonable dose. I had rented some movies and bought some frozen food, expecting to be at home for the day. I watched the first movie without noticing much effect. I felt kind of tired, but this may be because I was just being lazy. My stomach felt a little funky and none of the food in the house was appetizing. I decided to order a pizza for delivery, something mild, just a veggie. Thought about taking some more, but figured I should eat first, stomach being funky and all. I started the next movie. I did not realize just how stoned I was getting until I had to get up and pay the pizza guy, who turned out to be a pizza chick. I had a hard time even conversing with her.

"Not feeling like eating, I sat back down. When I closed my eyes I could visualize things. It is kind of hard to explain, but it was like I could very vividly daydream and visualize things. I also noticed a change in my physical sensations. I was bending my toes in the carpet and enjoying the feel. From then on I was kind of in my little world. I could not tell you about the movie or movies I watched.

"I don't really know about the time, but looking back the experience must have lasted a few hours. Up until this point, aside from my stomach, the experience was enjoyable. I then felt tired and like I had just come down from drinking a lot. Wanting to sleep, but edgy or something. Eventually I crashed. Looking back, I might try it again, but only if I had something for the comedown, like Vicodin or something."

Friend's Significant Other Describes Nutmeg Experience

"The ground nutmeg was incredibly difficult to get down. It took about two hours for me to notice an effect. I don't know if that had to do with the dose I took, or if that is typical. Once they came on, the effects seemed very similar to that of smoking marijuana. Like with marijuana, my eyes became red and I had cotton mouth. I became introspective and had some interesting insights. I then had some incredible munchies. These were much greater than even bud produced. Lots of things seemed funny, just like being stoned. The really down side was the hangover. For two days my stomach was messed up and I did not feel right. There were some positive aspects to the whole thing, but I will stick with marijuana or just about anything else in the future. Thanks."

Some Risks of Using Nutmeg

The majority opinion is that it is unlikely that one can die from an overdose of nutmeg. However, a review of the literature uncovers one report of a death that appears likely due to nutmeg, and one death that may be due to an interaction between nutmeg and another drug.

The first case involves an eight-year-old boy who ingested

a large amount of nutmeg for his small size (approximately 14 grams). He died within one day. Doctors concluded that the only explanation for his death that they could find was an overdose on nutmeg.

The second case involved a woman who took Rohypnol (flunitrazepam), often referred to as the "date rape drug," with a large dose of nutmeg and subsequently died. Doctors concluded that the amount of Rohypnol could not alone cause death, so the combination of it with nutmeg must have resulted in her death.

Given the large number of people who have used nutmeg, and that only two possible deaths have been related to it, one wonders if large doses of nutmeg can lead to death. At the same time, there may be the possibility that taking large amounts of nutmeg or mixing it with other drugs could result in death.

In addition to the two fatalities mentioned above, there are several documented cases of people coming to emergency rooms following ingestion of large amounts of nutmeg. In all the cases I researched, the results of medical examination indicated no physiological damage caused by nutmeg ingestion.

A concern has been raised that one of the chemicals in nutmeg (myristicin) could damage the liver. Research so far has not supported such a conclusion, and there is even evidence that it may have the effect of protecting the liver from harm.

As was discussed earlier in this chapter, the FDA has classified one of the chemicals in nutmeg (safrole) as carcinogenic. There has also been concern that the chemical myristicin, which is contained in nutmeg and is similar to safrole, may be carcinogenic. The cancer-causing activity of both these chemicals has been debated, so those who partake of nutmeg are left to draw their own conclusions. No studies examining the connection between nutmeg use and cancer are available.

Further research is needed to determine whether there may be any negative effects from long-term, repeated use of nutmeg.

Aside from the above risks, there is always the possibility that someone will have an unusual sensitivity to nutmeg. The addiction potential for nutmeg appears to be low. The impairment resulting from nutmeg intoxication may also put a user at risk for harm.

CHAPTER 13

LEAVES OF THE SHEPHERDESS:
Salvia Divinorum
(Pastora, Shepherdess's Herb, Maria Pastora,
Yerba de Maria, Sally-D)

Description and History

Salvia divinorum is a psychoactive plant in the *Labiatae* family, which is also known as the mint family. Salvia is a type of sage.

An interesting thing about *Salvia divinorum* is that, with one exception, it has never been identified in the wild. All sources of it are being grown by people. This fact has led some researchers to conclude that it is a hybrid developed by indigenous people in Mexico. The one place where it has been found growing seemingly wild is in a few ravine locations in the Sierra Mazateca mountains in Oaxaca, Mexico. Many botanists believe that *Salvia divinorum* is a cultigen (i.e., a cultivated plant that does not have a wild or uncultivated counterpart, like a banana). It is not known to exist in the wild, and the few patches that are known in the Sierra Mazateca appear to be the result of deliberate planting.

The first written mention of this plant was probably by J. B. Johnson in 1939. Johnson, along with a group of young anthropologists, visited the Mazatec town of Huautla de Jiminéz in Oaxaca. He wrote articles about Mazatec culture and language. Johnson was probably the first anthropologist to observe and write about the use of psychedelic mushrooms by indigenous people in Mexico. He also wrote about the use of a plant he called "hierba Maria," now identified as *Salvia divinorum*. In 1952, Robert Weitlaner described a Mexican ceremony that featured the use of "yerba de Maria," most likely *Salvia divinorum*.

Between 1953 and 1962, R. Gordon Wasson and his colleagues made several trips to the highlands of the southern Mexican state of Oaxaca to study the religious use of hallucinogenic mushrooms by the people there. Wasson described a plant used by the people when the psychotropic mushrooms were not available. He and his companions brought back specimens of the plant. The first samples were not adequate for identification, but in October 1962, they obtained a sample that they were able to identify as a new species of *Salvia* (sage). They labeled the plant *Salvia divinorum*. The plant was being used by the Mazatec Indians as part of their traditional divination rites.

The Mazatecs informed Wasson that the plants do not flower or produce seeds. They grew the plants by taking a shoot from an existing plant and placing it in the ground. The Mazatecs told Wasson that the plant must be placed in black soil, rather than clay, and that the plants must receive steady moisture. Most of the Mazatec families had their own garden of the plants, but the gardens were usually not near homes or trails, so that passers-by would not see them.

The Mazatecs called *Salvia divinorum* "hojas de la Pastora" (leaves of the Shepherdess), or "hojas de Maria Pastora" (leaves of Mary the Shepherdess). Maria (Mary) probably refers to the Virgin Mary of Christianity, but the reference to her as a shepherdess probably comes from some pre-Christian religion.

In the 1980s or early 1990s, B. Blosser obtained a strain of *Salvia divinorum* from Mexico. It has been described as having a less bitter taste than the strain Wasson obtained. Two strains make up most, if not all, of the *Salvia* currently available on the market. These two strains have been labeled the Blosser, being that obtained by Blosser, and the Wasson/Hoffman, believed to be from that obtained by Wasson.

The belief that this second strain was from Wasson's samples has been consistently reported in the literature and trade of *Salvia divinorum*. In 2003, Daniel Siebert reported in the Winter Solstice edition of *The Entheogen Review* that the source of the Wasson strain was not from the 1962 specimens collected by Wasson. Siebert reported that several correspondences by Wasson clearly indicate that the specimens he obtained were all dried prior to being brought back with him and that they could not have been planted.

Siebert stated that the actual source of the so-called Wasson strain is a psychiatrist and ecologist named Sterling Bunnell. Bunnell traveled to Sierra Mazateca with poet and playwright Michael McClure in June 1962. Bunnell obtained live plants of *Salvia divinorum* from a Mazateca curandero named Isauro Nave. He brought the specimens back to California and

planted them at his home. He subsequently supplied specimens to the University of California, Berkeley (UCB), and the
University of California, Los Angeles (UCLA), as well as to the
researcher Alexander Shulgin.

It was this plant, which was made available at the same
time as Wasson published his report on *Salvia divinorum*, that
has been labeled the Wasson strain. Despite its more properly
being labeled the Bunnell strain, it continues to be sold and
identified as the Wasson/Hoffman strain.

Another interesting article by Daniel Siebert was published
in *The Entheogen Review,* Autumnal Equinox, 2005. It provided a theory as to why the long history of *Salvia divinorum*
use in Mexico was unknown until relatively recently. It took
until almost the middle of the nineteenth century for the rest
of the world to discover *Salvia divinorum*, despite its long history of use by indigenous people in Mexico. Siebert reported
that Mazatec shamans have grown *Salvia divinorum* only in
hidden locations and have rarely discussed it with anyone outside their culture.

He argues that this secretiveness resulted from the history
of persecution of Native Americans beginning with the Spanish explorers and the seventeenth-century Catholic Church. In
1620, the Holy Office of the Inquisition in Mexico City made
the use of inebriating plants a heresy. Punishment for their
use was severe and could even involve torture or death. Siebert
asserts that similar forms of persecution continued through
the centuries, giving the Native Americans a justified fear of
sharing the secrets of their sacred plants.

The threat of persecution continues to the current day with
the present drug war. Several countries and several states in

the United States have already begun the prosecution of those who wish to benefit from use of this mystical plant. It may only be a matter of time until the Mazateca shamans' fears become realized and they are once again punished for use of their sacred plant spirit guides.

An article published in 1994 by Leander Valdes in the *Journal of Psychoactive Drugs* described the traditional use of *Salvia divinorum*. He reported that the herb is "used by Mazatec curanderos for its hallucinogenic effects. They believe it allows them to travel to heaven and talk to God and the Saints about divination, diagnosis, and healing. It is reputed to be weaker than both the morning glory seeds and the various species of mushrooms. Thus, it is often the first of the three psychotropic plants employed in the training of future shamans."

Aside from its use for shamanic and recreational purposes, *Salvia divinorum* has also been investigated as a possible treatment for depression. Australian psychologist Karl Hanes reported to the author that he first began to consider the possibility that *Salvia divinorum* may have antidepressant effects after a patient described a significant decrease in depressive symptoms after self-administering the plant. Additional anecdotal reports of its healing of treatment-resistant depression led him to try using it with patients who had not responded to other available treatment modalities. He introduced *Salvia divinorum* to six patients and was able to gather follow-up information from all but one. Patients orally ingested the leaves of the plant multiple times a week. This initial series of case studies provided support for the long-lasting antidepressant effects of *Salvia divinorum*.

Unfortunately, the illegalization of *Salvia divinorum* in

Australia brought an end to Dr. Hanes's research. One must be cautious about putting a lot of weight on such a small study without the use of a placebo, or other research rigors, despite the promising implications. It is to be hoped that someone will conduct a well-constructed, large-scale study before the governments of the world all follow Australia's example.

In addition to examining the effects of the regular use of relatively small amounts of *Salvia divinorum* as was done by Dr. Hanes, the use of a single, or more, large doses of concentrated *Salvia* should also be examined. Previous studies of LSD and psilocybin have shown the therapeutic benefit of a small number of intensely psychedelic experiences. The short-term, intense effects of concentrated *Salvia divinorum* may lead to similar benefits. The short length of the effects may also reduce some of the negative effects that occur from the long-lasting effects of many other psychedelics.

Its short-term effects also allow for one to quickly come down from the substance if necessary. The use of pure salvinorin A, which is the chemical mainly responsible for the plant's psychoactive effects, would also allow for a well-controlled dose administration and the ability to continue the experience or end it quickly.

Low doses of *Salvia divinorum* typically produce more effects when one's eyes are closed than when they are open. High dosages usually produce intense visual effects with the eyes open or closed. The closed-eye effects of smaller doses have led many individuals to use it to enhance daydreaming, visualizations, and even sleep dreaming.

It has also been frequently used to enhance meditation, and

an increasing number of people are using it with their meditation practice. Such usage has led to some small studies to examine more precisely what, if any, effects it has on meditation. Ian Soutar and Rick Strassman, M.D., conducted studies on *Salvia divinorum* and meditation in 1999 and 2000. Their work was subsequently reported by the Multidisciplinary Association of Psychedelic Studies (MAPS).

The active ingredient in their study was chewed leaves of *Salvia divinorum* ranging from 0.5 grams to 2 grams. The researchers had difficulty determining a suitable placebo substance. One reasonable option was using comfrey with quinine sulphate added for bitterness. A species of nettles also provided a fairly good placebo. The results of their small study demonstrated that *Salvia divinorum* had beneficial effects for meditation when compared to placebo or using nothing. A dosage of 1 gram of chewed leaves seemed to work well for most participants. Some participants preferred a dosage of 1.5 grams, especially if music was playing, but others found it too intense. A dosage of 0.5 grams had too little or no effect, and a dosage of 2 grams was too intense to allow effective meditation. There is more information on dosages later in this chapter.

The beneficial effects of *Salvia divinorum* on meditation included clearer and more focused thoughts, near-elimination of distracting thoughts and worries, and an overall calming effect. The duration of the positive effect on meditation was about one hour.

Unlike most species of *Salvia* (sage), *Salvia divinorum* produces few seeds, and the seeds that it does produce seldom germinate. As a result, the plant is almost exclusively grown by taking cuttings and growing them. Because the plant must be grown from cuttings, all known specimens are clones from a small number of collected plants from the original two strains. There may exist some additional strains, but there has not been any information at this point that indicates they are much different from the original two.

In 1980, a bioassay-directed investigation of the plant was undertaken to determine the chemical, or chemicals, responsible for *Salvia divinorum*'s effects. One chemical, labeled salvinorin A, was determined to be the primary cause of the plant's psychoactive effects. A second chemical, labeled salvinorin B, was also identified, but it does not appear to have any psychoactive effects.

Though salvinorin A is the chemical primarily responsible for *Salvia divinorum*'s effects, another chemical discovered by Leander J. Valdes III may also contribute to its effects. Valdes named this chemical divinorin C. Based on testing on mice, he estimated that divinorin C is responsible for about 10 percent of the psychoactive effects of *Salvia divinorum*. Even though this more recently discovered chemical is the lesser of the two psychoactive components, it appears to be more potent than the same amount of salvinorin A. Additional support for the theory that divinorin C has psychoactive properties comes from a few subjective reports that the effects of pure salvinorin A differ from the effects of *Salvia divinorum* in its whole form. Research is needed on divinorin C to determine whether it is active in humans and not just mice.

When I started this book in 2004, *Salvia divinorum* was legal throughout the United States and in most countries (Australia being one of the exceptions). By the time this book was completed, the legal status of *Salvia divinorum* had begun to change, though it still remains legal in most places. In the United States, Delaware, Missouri, Louisiana, Oklahoma, North Dakota, Tennessee, Kansas, Virginia, and Illinois have all passed laws making *Salvia divinorum* illegal.

An interesting part of the Kansas and Illinois laws is that they make illegal "any extract from any part of the plant, and every compound, manufacture, salts, isomers, and salts of isomers . . . derivative, mixture, or preparation of the plant, its seeds or extracts." The absurdity of this law is that it is so broad that it makes water, chlorophyll, cellulose, and many other contents of plants illegal.

On May 15, 2007, a Maine law went into effect that made it illegal to sell *Salvia divinorum* to minors, but it remained legal for adults. In October 2002, a bill was introduced to the United States Congress proposing that *Salvia divinorum* and salvinorin A be placed on Schedule I of the Controlled Substance Act. This proposal would have made it illegal to buy, sell, possess, or use *Salvia divinorum*. Luckily, the bill died without ever making it to a congressional vote.

At the time of this writing, the DEA is examining *Salvia divinorum* and salvinorin A to determine if they present a significant enough risk to public safety that they should be a controlled substance. The Controlled Substances Act requires that the DEA conduct an analysis of a substance prior to declaring it a controlled substance. The DEA considers eight factors in making this assessment:

1. Its potential for abuse
2. Its historical and current pattern of abuse

3. The duration, scope, and significance of abuse
4. The risk of psychological or physical dependence
5. Scientific information on its pharmacological effects
6. The state of current scientific knowledge about the substance/drug
7. Its risk, if any, to public health
8. Whether or not it is a precursor to a controlled substance

Internationally, Australia, Belgium, Denmark, Italy, and South Korea have all passed laws against its use. Spain prohibits the sale of *Salvia divinorum,* but not its possession or use. In Finland, Norway, Iceland, and Estonia, it is illegal to import it without a doctor's prescription. Several websites track the legal status of the plant. Here are a few of these websites that seem to keep pretty current:

www.sagewisdom.org/legalstatus.html
www.salvia.net/en/legality.htm
www.erowid.org/plants/salvia/salvia_law.shtml

In addition, a Yahoo! group devoted to all issues related to *Salvia divinorum* is located at groups.yahoo.com/group/salviaD.

Chemistry and Physiological Effects

The chemical responsible for *Salvia divinorum*'s effects is salvinorin A. Testing of salvinorin A indicated that it had activity and potency similar to that of mescaline. Salvinorin A is not soluble in water. Salvinorin A is inactive if taken orally. The compound is effective in doses of 200 to 500 mcg when smoked in a manner similar to cocaine free base. Salvinorin A seems to vaporize quickly when heated.

A dissertation by Thomas Anthony Munro, dated April 2006, at the University of Melbourne, Department of Chemistry, titled "The Chemistry of *Salvia divinorum*," provides a thorough review of the scientific information regarding *Salvia divinorum*. The complete text is available online at www.eprints.infodiv.unimelb.edu.au/archive/00002327/01/Mun ro2006thesis.pdf.

Based on studies of the effects of inhaled salvinorin A, it has a half-life of less than five minutes (i.e., at least half of the substance is removed from the body five minutes after inhaling it). Studies on swallowing salvinorin A show no effect, indicating that it is not psychoactive when ingested. However, it does have an effect when held in the lip (in the same manner that chewing tobacco is used), allowing it to be absorbed through the oral mucosa.

Little is known regarding how salvinorin A affects the brain to cause its psychoactive effects. There is also a lack of information on how salvinorin A is metabolized.

How People Obtain and Use *Salvia divinorum*

The effect of a *Salvia divinorum* high is going to be totally dependent upon how much salvinorin A is in an individual's bloodstream. There are four ways that people use *Salvia divinorum*:

1. Chewing the fresh leaves
2. Smoking the dried leaves
3. Smoking an extract
4. Using pure salvinorin A

Chewing the fresh leaves and smoking the dried leaves will both produce fairly mild effects. When the herb *Salvia divinorum* is consumed either by smoking the dried leaf or chewing the fresh leaves, the effects are usually pleasant and interesting. When used this way, the amount of salvinorin A absorbed into the bloodstream is usually very small, and in the case of the chewed leaves, it is absorbed into the bloodstream gradually.

The inebriation at low doses can resemble that of a mild marijuana high in certain ways. At higher doses, it resembles hallucinogenic states like LSD and psilocybin. At still higher doses it may resemble disassociative states such as ketamine produces.

Smoking an extract and taking pure salvinorin A will both produce very intense effects. The only source of pure salvinorin A that I was able to locate was from Daniel Siebert at the Salvia Divinorum Research and Information Center. He sells the pure chemical only to "qualified scientists involved in legitimate scientific research." As a clinical psychologist intending to do legitimate research on the use of *Salvia divinorum* for treating depression, I attempted to contact him for information on purchasing salvinorin A, but did not hear back from him. It appears that he has provided salvinorin A for research before, but it is unclear if he is still willing to do so. Siebert is a major advocate for keeping *Salvia divinorum* legal, and his website located at www.sagewisdom.org contains a wealth of information on the plant and its legal status.

The chemistry involved in creating pure salvinorin A is very complex; therefore, the methods of use discussed below are chewing the fresh leaves, smoking the dried leaves, and smoking an extract (which is the method used by most people seeking the salvinorin A effect). However, if one is interested in the chemistry of obtaining pure salvinorin A, one might try entering into an internet search engine "extracting pure salvinorin A," or go to the following:

> www.entheology.org/edoto/anmviewer.asp?a=4&z=6
> www.totse.com/en/drugs/miscellaneous_drug_
> information/extractingsalv171808.html

Chewing the Fresh Leaves

To obtain the fresh leaves will typically involve growing the plant yourself. There are many places to obtain fresh *Salvia divinorum* plants. Many people sell them on eBay, and doing an Internet search for live plants will bring up many sources. Here are a couple of good sources for live plants:

> www.salvialight.com
> www.greenstranger.com
> www.bouncingbearbotanicals.com

Growing *Salvia divinorum* is fairly easy. Any general purpose fertilizer will work fine, but don't overfeed the plants. They respond well to regular feeding, but they seem sensitive to excess fertilizer and will put out deformed growth if overfed. The plants need a lot of room for their roots, so they should be re-potted to larger pots every few months if they are growing quickly. They grow best in light shade with no more than five or six hours of sun. On the other hand, they do not do well in deep shade. The stems of *Salvia divinorum* are not very strong, and they will usually need some sort of support to keep them from breaking. They can be grown outdoors, provided that the above conditions are met.

The *Salvia Divinorum Growers Guide,* by Sociedad Para La Preservation De Las Plartes Del Mister and Richard G. Goire, provides suggestions on protecting *Salvia divinorum* plants from pests. The book recommends preparing a solution of four parts water, one part rubbing alcohol, and one part liquid soap. The solution is then applied to the plants to eliminate and protect the plants from damaging pests.

Even though *Salvia divinorum* does not typically produce seeds, it is relatively easy to propagate. Small cuttings will usually root within two or three weeks. Cuttings seem to root best when they are between two and eight inches long. They should be cut from the mother plant using sharp, clean shears. The cut should be made just below a node. Cuttings should be placed into a cup of water until they sprout roots, which takes a couple of weeks. After they have some roots, they can then be planted into pots with loose potting soil. Plants should be kept extra moist for the first few days after being planted because they will wilt in the first several days if in a dry environment. If this is a problem, placing some loose plastic wrap over the top of the pot to keep the water in may help.

Though *Salvia divinorum* does not produce seeds very frequently, and the seeds that are produced often will not grow, there are an increasing number of reports of people having some variable success with growing the plant from seed. When the plants are pollinated naturally or by hand, a small amount of them may produce seeds. Reports of attempts to germinate these seeds report a success rate between about 10 and 30 percent. Of those that germinate, about 15 to 35 percent will grow into healthy plants. This makes growing by seeds unreliable and often frustrating, but is an option for those willing to go through the trouble.

Germination of the seeds is done by placing them between damp paper towels, or by putting them just below the surface of potting soil (sometimes mixed with peat moss) and keeping them damp. They need enough water to germinate, but too much water may harm the seeds. Some plants from seeds grow as well as those from cuttings, but of those that survive, many have shorter roots, weaker stems, and slower growth.

People use fresh *Salvia divinorum* leaf by chewing them in what is called a quid. This is a traditional method of using it, but most people find this method unpleasant. The leaves taste bad, and some people vomit. People who use this method take about eight leaves and fold them together. They then chew these leaves and try to place them in the lower lip, or under the tongue. The individual will try to hold the juices in the mouth for as long as possible, but eventually will spit the juice out. This is similar to chewing tobacco. The goal is to get as much salvinorin A as possible absorbed by the membranes in the front lip or under the tongue. After getting most of the juice out of these leaves, the person takes more leaves and does the same thing over again.

Smoking the Dried Leaves

This method involves purchasing dried *Salvia divinorum* leaves and smoking them in a pipe (e.g., a pipe like marijuana is smoked in). A bong, hookah, or any other smoking implement can be used. Salvinorin A vaporizes quickly, so the first hit will be stronger than subsequent hits. One can buy dried leaves from eBay or by doing an Internet search. Following are some good sources for dried *Salvia divinorum* leaves:

www.salvia-divinorum.com
www.iamshaman.com
www.giftsfromtheancients.com
www.ethnobotanicals.com
www.shamanshop.com
www.salviaonline.co.uk
www.mazatecgarden.com

Smoking an Extract

This is the most common method that people use to get an intense salvinorin A experience. Because salvinorin A is vaporized quickly, the first hit off of a pipe with the extract in it is going to be much more intense than following hits. This is different from the experience of marijuana smokers, who get several hits off of the same pipe of bud. Salvinorin A extract smokers typically take the first hit and hold it for as long as possible. If they are not too far gone, they then take a second hit. This use removes most of the salvinorin A, so the next person empties out the pipe and refills it for him or herself.

Salvia divinorum extracts are described in relation to their concentrations. Typical concentrations are 5×, 10×, and 20×. This refers to how concentracted the active ingredient (salvinorium A), is. Obviously, 20× is the most concentrated.

Go to any Internet search engine to look for *Salvia divinorum* extracts. Here are a few good sources:

www.giftsfromtheancients.com
www.salviadivinorum.com
www.iamshaman.com
www.ethnobotanicals.com
www.shamanshop.com
www.salviaonline.co.uk
www.mazatecgarden.com

The *Salvia divinorum* Experience

The effects of *Salvia divinorum* depend on how much of the active chemical salvinorin A enters the system. Low doses produce a slight buzz similar to that experienced after smoking a small amount of marijuana. Higher doses, such as smoking a 20× extract produces an intense psychedelic experience.

The onset of effect from smoking occurs within several seconds. Feeling like one has been transferred into another world is a common experience. Visual hallucinations and distortion of objects being viewed are typical. The body often feels weighed down. Most people report that the experience is pleasurable, or at least not unpleasant.

Though the effects can be intense, they quickly fade away

in two to ten minutes, returning the person back to reality before they can become too uncomfortable. Despite the short duration, a small amount of people report feeling anxious or even panicky due to the intensity.

Weightlifting Friend Tries Salvia divinorum

[After taking one hit of *Salvia divinorum* 20× extract and holding the hit as long as possible]

"It felt euphoric and then relaxing. Then I started to giggle and have a spacy feeling. This lasted for about five to ten minutes. Looking back at the experience, I can't to put words to it."

Thirty-something Psychotherapist Tries Salvia divinorum *Extract*

[After taking one hit of *Salvia divinorum* 20× extract and holding the hit as long as possible]

"After about twenty seconds, before breathing out, I felt a numbness over my body. Everything began to change, as if I were in a different place. Around this point I exhaled. The hair of the two women across from me appeard to form into a red fence. The fence moved closer to my eyes, and I was no longer aware of what was happening in the room around me. I do not know if my eyes were open or closed, but I was no longer seeing what was happening around me.

"I continued in this state for about two minutes. Despite being removed from reality, I felt euphoric. No sense of being afraid. Gradually the people around me came back into my vision. I began to realize once again were I was. A pleasant contentment lasted for another twenty minutes, and then it faded out over the next half hour."

The Same Psychotherapist Tries Salvia divinorum Extract Again

[After taking two hits of *Salvia divinorum* 20× extract and holding the hit as long as possible]

"It came on right away. It felt like someone was pulling me. My perception was definitely distorted, like everything was flattened out. Like I got pulled up and everything was getting flattened, which is a real weird feeling. It took like five minutes for my perception to become more normal. I almost disassociated a bit."

Psychotherapist's Friend Describes First Salvia divinorum Experience

[Smoking dried *Salvia divinorum* leaf]

"I felt like someone was pushing me down. Pushing me down from my shoulders and then trying to make me lay down. It lasted for about fifteen seconds."

Artist and Frequent Salvia divinorum User Describes Experience

[After smoking 15× extract, used multiple times]

"Instantly, when you breathe it, it brings you into a dream world. This substance is pretty strange stuff. It enhances me artistically. If used at home safely *Salvia divinorum* is like mushrooms for five to ten minutes, but then it leaves you with a pleasant feeling. It has enhanced some art I do tremendously. The beauty this thing can produce is unbelievable, with no after-effect."

Some Risks of Using *Salvia divinorum*

No information is available regarding the risks of using *Salvia divinorum* or salvinorin A. The effects of taking a high dose of salvinorin A are so intense that a user could do something dangerous. In fact, the dangers that are present when anyone uses a mind-altering substance should be considered. This drug is so intense that addiction is unlikely. Using a concentrated form of *Salvia divinorum*, like a 20x extract, could result in what is commonly called a "bad trip," and this writer has heard of a couple such experiences. Due to the fact that the experience ends so quickly (usually within several minutes), the risk of "bad trips" is much less severe than it is with most other psychedelic substances.

CHAPTER 14

SAINT OF THE CURANDEROS:
San Pedro Cactus
(*Trichocereus pachanoi,* Achuma, Wachuma, Huachuma)

Description and History

The San Pedro cactus *(Trichocereus pachanoi)* contains the hallucinogenic substance mescaline. Mescaline is the psychoactive chemical in the better known cactus peyote. Peyote's popularity has led to its being made illegal in the United States. The San Pedro cactus is less well known, and thus it is still legal, though the chemical it contains (mescaline) is not legal. Due to the illegal status of mescaline, a user faces criminal charges if authorities can determine the person is growing or utilizing San Pedro cacti for the purpose of getting high from the mescaline.

The San Pedro cactus is a fast-growing, columnar cactus. Aside from peyote, it is the best-known source of naturally occurring mescaline (meaning that it has more mescaline than any other natural source). The majority of the mescaline is contained in the outer half-inch of its skin. It is native to the

Andes of Peru and Ecuador, but it is able to grow in many places.

The San Pedro cactus is light to dark green with spines located evenly at nodes approximately two centimeters apart. The cactus can grow up to fifteen feet tall, with multiple branches. It is easy to grow and it can be grown from seed. The plant is used to the harsh, cold environment of the Andes, making it more able to tolerate cold than many other cactus varieties.

A South American stone carving dating from 1300 BC shows a figure holding up what appears to be sections of the San Pedro cactus. The carving belongs to the Chavin culture, and it was found in the northern highlands of Peru. Moche (an early Peruvian civilization) statues, which date from the time of Christ, appear to depict the San Pedro cactus. The name San Pedro refers to the Catholic Saint Peter. The cactus was probably used as part of the shamanic rituals of the native people when the Spaniards arrived in South America. The integration of the natives with the Catholic Spaniards probably resulted in the cactus being called San Pedro.

Despite the Catholic Spaniard influence, the San Pedro cactus "religion" has continued. One prominent shaman is Juan Navarro, who comes from a long history of healers and shamans. He was born in the village of Somate and first ingested San Pedro at the age of eight. He now works with his two sons performing invocations, divination, and healings, using a variety of objects called "artes." These artes are sacred and include shells, magnets, crystals, swords, rocks from the stomachs of animals, and objects resembling sexual organs.

Some of these objects are from pre-Columbian tombs, and Navarro believes they have magical powers.

In addition to the San Pedro cactus, several other varieties of the *Trichocerei* family are also psychoactive. *Trichocerei pachanoi* has been reported to contain at least 2 percent to 3 percent mescaline. *Trichocereus bridgesii* is reported to be a potent form of this variety of cactus. *Trichocereus bridgesii forma monstruosa* is a similar cactus that is also reported to be psychoactive. *Trichocereus macrogonus* is also described as psychoactive, but with a potency less than that of *Trichocereus bridgesii*. A couple of other varieties worth considering are *Trichocereus peruvianus* (Peruvian Torch) and *Trichocereus terscheckii* (Cardon Grande).

Chemistry and Physiological Effects

The psychoactive ingredient in the San Pedro cactus is mescaline. Thus, the information provided here will be about mescaline. Mescaline is a phenethylamine that was first identified by Arthur Heffter in 1897. Its chemical name is 3,4,5-trimethoxybenzeneethanamine. Mescaline, like LSD, is active at serotonin receptor sites. Specifically, it is an agonist at 5HT2A and 5HT2 receptor sites. Through its action at these sites, it also affects glutamate, which is a chemical involved in nerve cell transmission.

Metabolic studies of mescaline show that the majority of it is excreted unchanged in the urine. Some of mescaline (which is chemically 3,4,5-trimethoxybenzeneethanamine) is converted to 3,4,5-trimethoxyphenylacetic acid.

Physiological Effects of Mescaline

increased heart rate

increased blood pressure

elevated body temperature

dilation of the pupils

reduced coordination

How People Obtain and Use San Pedro Cactus

One problem people have with using San Pedro cactus as a psychoactive is that the amount of mescaline present in the cactus varies. Some samples that have been examined have yielded mescaline percentages ranging from approximately 0.02 percent to 0.12 percent. The average psychoactive dose of mescaline has been estimated at 200 to 500 milligrams. These numbers would allow one to calculate the amount of San Pedro that would make an average psychoactive dose, if one knew the percentage of mescaline in a given sample of the cactus.

It is unlikely that someone using San Pedro cactus is going to know the percentage of mescaline in their sample. This means that they have to estimate the amount needed and learn from experience. The lethal dose, based on rat studies, is much higher than the psychoactive dose. It is estimated at approximately 370 milligrams per kilogram of the person's weight. This means that for a 150 (68.18 kg)-pound person, the average lethal dose would be approximately 25,226 milligrams. In other words, one would have to eat a heck of a lot of San Pedro cactus to overdose on mescaline.

Typing "buy san pedro cactus" into any Internet search

engine will result in several sources for purchasing the plant. People buy the whole living cactus, they buy cuttings from the cactus, and they buy seeds to grow the cactus. Here are a few sources for San Pedro cactus plants, seeds, and cuttings:

www.giftsfromtheancients.com
www.bouncingbearbotanicals.com
www.psychoactiveherbs.com
www.herbalfire.com

The San Pedro cactus is commonly purchased for ornamental use by people totally unaware of its mind-altering properties, and it is commonly available in nurseries and other stores that sell plants. Some of the best prices for the cactus have been found at Target and Home Depot.

In order to deter people from ingesting them, it is often reported that many commercial growers of San Pedro cactus add poisons to the plant that can make a user sick. This is a common practice with commercially sold morning glory seeds, but I was not able to verify if this practice was also common with San Pedro. To be safe, one could buy cactus only from those who specialize in selling ethnobotanicals. One could also buy San Pedro cacti from a mainstream nursery and use it only as plant stock for growing chemical-free San Pedro cacti of one's own.

To grow San Pedro cactus, here are a few things to be aware of:

• The cactus likes a lot of light.
• The plant does best in areas with long summers.
• The use of grow lights may help in areas that do not get a lot of sunshine.

- A very hardy cactus, San Pedro will probably survive in areas with less sunlight, but its rate of growth will be slower.
- The cactus prefers a very porous soil.
- A pre-prepared cactus soil mix is adequate, but adding a little pumice to the mix is even better.
- A wide pot is best for its roots. (A narrow pot, even if very deep, will stunt the growth of the cactus.)
- The pot should have good drainage.
- The cactus should be watered frequently, whenever the surface soil is dry.

Once the cactus is in hand, here are a couple ways to use and prepare it.

San Pedro Recipe 1

Remove the spines from a piece of San Pedro cactus between six and twelve inches long. Break it into pieces and grind the pieces in a blender or food processor. Place the ground cactus into a large pot and add enough water to cover it well. Boil the cactus for three hours. Add water as needed to keep it from running out of liquid. After the three hours, take a strainer and strain the liquid into a bowl, and save the liquid for later. Return the cactus pulp to the pot. Add some more water to cover it, then boil it again for another two hours or so, adding water as needed as before. Once again, strain off the water and save it. Discard the cactus pulp. The liquid then can be drunk as is, or it can be boiled longer to reduce the amount.

San Pedro Recipe 2

Remove the spines from a twelve-inch piece of San Pedro cactus. Slice the cactus into half-inch slices. Place the slices into a blender with enough water to just cover the cactus (it may take more than one blender full, depending on the size of your blender). Blend the cactus, then place into a large pot. The cactus will boil up some, so make sure the pot has plenty of room. Boil the cactus for about three to four hours. The stuff in the pot will foam up, so it has to be monitored so that it does not boil over. Make sure that the liquid does not boil off. More water can be added if needed.

Following the boil, the next step is to remove the liquid from the cactus pulp. The best way to do this is to let the stuff in the pot cool to the point it will not burn your hands. Then take a bowl large enough to hold the liquid and place a dish towel over it. Slowly pour the contents of the pot into the dish towel and strain the liquid into the bowl. You will probably need an assistant to lift the sides of the towel so no liquid is lost. Once most of the liquid has strained through the towel, ball the towel up around the pulp and squeeze the remaining liquid out of it. One can drink the liquid as is, or boil it further to reduce the amount.

A Few Other Suggestions

The general opinion seems to be that the majority of mescaline is contained in the outer half inch of the plant. Therefore, one could probably remove the center of the cactus and discard

it, using only the outer half inch. One could also just eat the
outer half inch of the plant, as opposed to going through the
whole boiling process, but this can be hard on the stomach.
San Pedro cactus can often cause nausea. Some people have
recommended taking something that counteracts nausea, like
Dramamine or Pepto-Bismol.

Making a San Pedro Cactus Extract

It is important to note that the extract produced will contain
a relatively high dose of mescaline. Producing this extract may
cross the legal line from legally possessing the plant to illegally
possessing mescaline. Mescaline is clearly illegal in the United
States, but because the San Pedro cactus containing it is not,
the legality of a concentrated form of the plant is unclear. One
Internet report tells of an arrest for producing such an extract,
but this writer was not able to find any documentation to determine if this report was true or just fear-mongering. The site
www.clearwhitelight.org/hatter/extract.htm contains direc-
tions on producing fairly pure mescaline from the San Pedro
cactus. Clearly, producing mescaline in this way is illegal.

To produce the extract, begin by removing the spines and
outer skin from the cactus. One should then cut out the core
of the cactus, leaving just the outer half inch remaining. The
cored pieces should then be chopped into very small pieces
and placed in a jar. Pour into the jar enough Everclear or pure
drinking alcohol to cover the pieces. Place a lid on the jar. Allow the jar to sit for two to four weeks, shaking it at least once
a day. Some people recommend draining the alcohol off half-
way through the soaking period, setting it aside in a sealed

container, and then adding Everclear or pure drinking alcohol to the jar again.

The next step is to drain the alcohol off of the cactus and squeeze out any remaining liquid from the cactus. Strain all of the liquid with a cloth or coffee filter, including the previous alcohol drained off if this was done. This strained liquid can be used for the next step as is, or any remaining particles can be allowed to settle and then it can be decanted to produce as particle-free a substance as possible. The remaining liquid is then placed in a flat cake pan or similar dish. This dish should be placed in front of a fan to evaporate the liquid. Make sure that the fan blows across the surface and is not on so high that it splashes anything out of the pan. What remains will be the gooey San Pedro cactus extract, ready for use or storage. Some people add a little bit of Everclear or pure drinking alcohol to make a sort of tincture.

The substance should be kept in a cool, dark place. It should keep its potency for at least a few weeks to months, but the exact length of time it remains potent needs to be determined. Due to variations in potency, it is difficult to know what the proper dosage for use should be. Determining the ratio of extract to plant material used should give an idea of how potent it is relative to the unaltered material. Starting small is the usual guideline.

Some Other Methods of Using San Pedro Cactus

In addition to the above methods of using San Pedro, some reports have been recorded of people using the cactus by inhaling it nasally and by placing it into capsules and swallowing them. In order to get enough of the psychoactive chemical by either of these methods, one would probably need to use a concentrated extract. The amount of material needed makes nasal use impossible without using an extract. Placing the ground cactus into capsules would make it possible to use the pure San Pedro cactus, but the number of capsules to produce an effect would be difficult to swallow. Using an extract would greatly reduce the number of capsules needed. Using capsules of the extract may also reduce nausea.

The most unusual method of using San Pedro cactus, or any other natural product, that I have come across, is by enema. In the Summer Solstice, 2004, issue of *The Entheogen Review,* an article by Justin Case, Fun Gal, and R. Stuart described what they called "The Enema Project." Their method began with chopping the cactus into very small pieces. One would probably want to remove the spines, skin, and center of the cactus first. The substance was then placed in a pot with water and allowed to simmer for two to three hours. After it cooled, they strained the mixture with a colander and straining bag and set the liquid aside. They repeated this three more times, and they then boiled each of the collections separately to reduce the volume. It is unclear why this was done separately, and one could probably just combine the liquid into one boil.

Once a thickened liquid was obtained, they placed it into emptied out enema bottles made by Fleet. Presumably, any type of enema bottle could be used. They noted that a little bit of air needed to be left in the bottle for the liquid to be easily expelled. All one has to do is empty the bowels as fully as possible, insert the enema, slowly squeeze in the liquid, try to lie on one's stomach and hold it in for two to three hours, and expel the remaining liquid into the toilet.

As far as dosage, the authors tried a variety of cacti at a range of doses, making it difficult to recommend the specific amount of San Pedro cactus to be used. They did note that their method produced milder effects than taking the same dosage orally.

As always, most people recommend starting small. It has also been suggested that adding some lemon juice or citric acid to the brew may help with extraction. It seems like a hard way to go for a psychedelic experience, but whatever works for you.

The San Pedro Cactus Experience

The onset of the San Pedro cactus experience begins about thirty minutes after ingestion. Onset is affected by the amount of food in the stomach, with a full stomach taking a little bit longer to produce an effect. Physical effects of nausea and muscle tension are common in the first thirty to sixty minutes. Vomiting usually relieves the nausea for the rest of the experience. These physical effects will eventually subside.

Visual effects are probably the most common part of the experience, but these are not experienced by all. Color effects, spirals, cobweb designs, halos, lattice designs, and other patterns are common. Perception of sound is altered, and music often seems intensified.

Individuals usually feel more introspective, and it is common to feel that one is having great insights into the nature of the universe.

Intense emotional experiences occur, and the emotions can become labile. People often experience intensely enjoyable feelings and insights, but some find the experience very upsetting. This negative response, commonly called a "bad trip," may involve intense anxiety and panic. People are more open to outside influence, and the setting where the cacti are used partially determines one's experience.

The experience peaks in around three hours. The main effect lasts six to eight hours. The after-effect, when one continues to feel mildly altered, is usually experienced up to the twelve- to fourteen-hour point.

Some Risks of Using San Pedro Cactus

Theoretically, it is possible to overdose on mescaline from taking San Pedro cactus. In reality, it would be so difficult to consume and hold down the amount of cactus necessary to overdose, that it is highly unlikely. This writer has not been able to find any reports of overdose on San Pedro cactus.

The most common negative effect of San Pedro cactus is nausea and vomiting. Muscle tightening is also sometimes reported. The possibility of a "bad trip" is another possible negative effect. Those who are already psychologically unstable or prone to psychosis are at risk for prolonged negative effects. Some data show that those individual taking insulin for diabetes should not take anything containing mescaline. Data also show that pregnant women should not take mescaline.

Opium Poppies
(Papaver somniferum)

Description and History

The opium poppy has been placed into an appendix, separate from the other chapters, because even though there are legal ways to grow it, law enforcement is likely to focus on those growing the poppy to produce opium. The exact legal status of possessing poppy seeds and poppy flowers is debatable, but law enforcement has generally not interfered with buying poppy seeds and growing poppies for ornamental purposes. Law enforcement has treated poppy seeds and poppy flowers as legal, though the law regarding them is unclear. Please note:

- It is illegal to produce opium or to even intend to produce it.
- It is illegal to possess opium or to ingest opium.
- It is illegal to possess or use any of the psychoactive chemicals contained in opium.

On the surface, its legal status is like that of ayahuasca or *Anadenathera* seeds, where the plant is legal, but the chemicals it contains are not. However, with the former two substances, the government rarely pursues legal action. With the opium poppy, the opposite is true. Law enforcement actively pursues cases of those trying to produce poppies. Having poppies growing in the yard is likely to draw suspicion if witnessed by a narcotics officer. Having poppies and a copy of this book is likely to be viewed as intent to produce opium.

Though one can obtain the means to produce opium legally, the likelihood of law enforcement action if they catch the slightest indication of your intent makes opium different from the other substances found in this book. I have received reports that some law enforcement agencies consider the growing of *Papaver somniferum* illegal regardless of the reason. This means that even the innocent growing of them for purely ornamental purposes could result in prosecution.

Trying to extract morphine from opium would just add to the crimes one has committed by gathering opium. The method for doing so will not be described here, but the book *Opium Poppy Garden: The Way of a Chinese Grower*, by William Griffith, describes how to produce morphine from opium.

An example that illuminates law enforcement's approach to those legally obtaining poppies or poppy seeds, whom they suspect of intending to make illegal opium, is the case of Jim Hogshire. In June 1994, Loompanics Unlimited published a book by Jim Hogshire titled *Opium for the Masses*.

This book informed its readers how they could legally buy opium poppy seeds and opium poppies. The book explains how to get the opium from the poppy pod and how to make opium tea from dried or fresh poppies. On March 6, 1996, a search warrant was served at Hogshire's apartment and he was arrested. Over a dozen Seattle police officers arrived at the apartment.

The events leading up to the arrest and search were reportedly started by a man named Robert Black. Black had contacted the Seattle police alleging that Jim Hogshire and his wife were involved in "narcotics activity" in their apartment. Black is a freelance writer who had been hired by a magazine to write an article about the Loompanics Unlimited publishing company. He contacted Loompanics, where someone suggested that he meet with Hogshire, because he had written books for Loompanics.

Jim and Heidi Hogshire agreed to meet with Black and on February 10, 1996, Heidi Hogshire picked up Black at the airport and drove him to her apartment, where he met Jim Hogshire. Black alleged that Jim Hogshire offered him opium tea, which he refused, and that Jim continually drank the opium tea himself. Black reported that Jim also took pills that he (Jim) claimed were Ritalin and snorted a powder he claimed was Dexedrine. Black reported that at approximately 2:00 a.m. on February 11, Jim pulled a gun on Black during an argument over religion and ordered him to leave. The Seattle police also reported other evidence that Hogshire may have at one point been in possession of chemicals that could be used to make either heroin or methamphetamine.

During the search of the Hogshires' residence in March 1996, Seattle police found a box containing approximately 2,200 grams of what they believed to be dried poppies. In addition, scales, weapons, pictures, and books were also seized.

Jim Hogshire was charged with possession of opium poppies with the intent of producing opium. The prosecution used Hogshire's book as evidence against him. This story does have a happy ending, though. The judge in the case rejected the prosecution's arguments and dismissed the charges against Jim Hogshire.

Use of opium from the poppy goes back at least as far as written history (i.e., approximately 6,000 years). The Sumerians in Mesopotamia (where writing first developed) wrote of cultivation of the opium poppy, which they called Hul Gil, the "joy plant." Ancient Egyptian hieroglyphics report the trade of opium poppies by 1300 BC, including during the reign of King Tutankhamen (King Tut).

The ancient Greeks and Romans made use of opium. Homer said that Helen of Troy served opium dissolved in wine. The Greek goddess Demeter is often associated with the opium poppy, and depictions of her commonly show her holding them. In 330 BC, Alexander the Great would bring opium to India and Persia. During the crusades, crusaders returned to Europe with opium, and during the Middle Ages, opium was commonly used. During the Renaissance, the doctor Paracelsus investigated the use of opium. He referred to it as his "stone of immortality," and he invented the use of opium laudanum. The poets Samuel Taylor Coleridge and Edger Allan Poe were frequent users of opium.

During the fifteenth and sixteenth centuries, the Dutch began purchasing opium from India. The British East India Company would eventually seek a monopoly on the opium trade, by forcing all Indian opium producers to sell only to them. By 1773, the British were bringing seventy-five tons of opium into their country. In 1803, a German named Friedrich Wilhelm Sertürner identified morphine as an active ingredient in opium.

In the first half of the 1800s, literary figures John Keats and Elizabeth Barrett Browning experimented with opium. Writer Thomas De Quincy published his autobiographical account of his opium use in 1821, titled *Confessions of an English Opium-Eater.*

In the mid-1800s, the Chinese rebelled against the British domination of the opium trade, resulting in the "Opium Wars." In March 1839, the Chinese commissioner Lin Zexu was appointed by the emperor to control the opium trade at the port of Canton. He immediately enforced the imperial demand that there be a permanent halt to drug shipments into China. When the British refused to end the trade, Lin imposed a trade embargo on the British.

On March 27, 1839, Charles Elliot, British Superintendent of Trade, demanded that all British subjects turn over opium to him, to be confiscated by Commissioner Lin Zexu, amounting to nearly a year's supply of the drug. Lin destroyed the opium that he received. The British responded by claiming that Lin and the Chinese had destroyed the personal property of British citizens.

In 1840, the British forces attacked. The British had superior technology that allowed them to defeat the Chinese. This first opium war lasted from 1840 to 1842, when the Treaty of Nanking was signed. The treaty required the Chinese to open several of their ports to British merchants again. It also made China pay millions of dollars to the British, and Hong Kong was ceded to the British.

After the first war, the opium trade continued, even though the treaty had not legalized it. In 1856, the Chinese again tried to stop the opium trade. The British and French attacked them, resulting in what has been called the second Opium War. In 1858, the war ended with the Treaty of Tientsin. This treaty gave the British and French the freedom to engage in the opium trade essentially legally. A huge amount of opium flooded into China, and addiction to opium was a major problem. The Chinese production of opium grew into a significant industry.

In the 1900s, scientists discovered how opium works. The opiates attach to receptors in the brain, called endorphin sites (for endogenous morphines). Our brain appears to have receptor sites that are ready to accept the opium molecule. The receptor sites for opium exist because the brain has a mechanism by which it releases its own opium-like chemicals called endorphins. Endorphins are peptides produced by the pituitary gland and the hypothalamus. Like the chemicals in opium, they have an analgesic (pain-reducing) effect, and they produce a feeling of well-being.

When Sertürner had isolated morphine from opium and discovered that it was a primary cause of opium's effects, his finding was a huge step forward for physicians with regard to pain control. Since the discovery of morphine, thirty-some other alkaloids have been isolated from opium. These alkaloids fall into two groups, phenanthrenes and benzylisquinolines. It is generally believed that only the phenanthrenes group of alkaloids, which includes morphine and codeine, contains chemicals that can produce a high. Many opiate-related substances have also been developed synthetically. In the mid-1800s the hypodermic needle became available. By injecting morphine, its pain-killing effects (as well as euphoric effects) could be felt rapidly.

The commonly used illicit drug heroin does not occur naturally in opium. It is a semi-synthetic opiate made by altering morphine. Heroin was first synthesized in 1874 by C. R. Alder Wright, an English chemist working at Saint Mary's Hospital Medical School in London, England. Wright was performing experiments combining morphine with different acids. He heated morphine and acetic anhydride for several hours to produce a more potent opiate he called diacetylmorphine (later called heroin).

Nothing would happen with heroin until twenty-three years later, when it was again synthesized by a chemist named Felix Hoffmann. Hoffmann worked for the Bayer pharmaceutical company in Germany. The head of the laboratory where Hoffmann worked was named Heinrich Dreser. Dreser instructed Hoffmann to acetylate morphine, with the intent of creating codeine. Instead of codeine, the diacetylmorphine previously made by Wright was produced. Bayer named the substance, which was about three times more potent than morphine, heroin.

In the late 1800s and early 1900s, heroin was marketed by Bayer as a treatment for coughs, pain, and tuberculosis. Bayer sold heroin as a non-addictive alternative to morphine, and it was marketed as a treatment for morphine addiction. It would subsequently be discovered that heroin is broken down into morphine by the body.

Chemistry and Physiological Effects

Opium contains more than thirty alkaloids. Morphine and codeine are two alkaloids that are responsible for much of opium's psychoactive and analgesic effects. The morphine that is available in the pharmaceutical market is in the forms of either morphine sulfate or morphine hydrochloride. Both appear as fine, white, odorless, crystalline powders and are described as having a bitter taste. They are both soluble in water and slightly soluble in alcohol.

As previously described, there are specific receptor sites in the central nervous system (called opioid receptors) to which morphine and other opiates attach. These receptor sites are present for the body's naturally occurring endorphins to attach to. Morphine is primarily metabolized into morphine-3-glucuronide (M3G) and morphine-6-glucuronide (M6G) via glucuronidation.

Codeine sold for medical purposes is produced in the forms of codeine sulfate, codeine hydrochloride, and codeine phosphate. Codeine has a relatively weak affinity for opiate receptors in the brain. However, a portion of codeine is converted to morphine by enzymes in the liver. This converted codeine probably has a greater effect on pain reduction than the codeine that is not converted to morphine.

Both morphine and codeine are central nervous system (CNS) depressants. They reduce blood pressure, heart rate, and respiration. They can interfere with urination, and constipation is a common effect. Both substances also depress pain. Codeine decreases the cough reflex.

Two other alkaloids contained in opium also have physiological effects. These substances are papaverine and thebaine. Papaverine is occasionally used as a medication to treat spasms of the gastrointestinal tract, bile ducts, and ureter. It is also used as a coronary vasodilator and as a smooth muscle relaxant. The exact mechanism of action for papaverine still needs to be examined, but it may act by inhibition of the phosphodiesterase enzymes and/or by altering mitochondrial respiration. Thebaine differs from most other opiates in that it has stimulating effects. It currently has no approved medical uses, but it is used to produce other opiates, such as hydrocodone and oxycodone.

How People Obtain and Use Opium Poppies

The illegal trade in opium, some of its alkaloids, and synthetic opiates is not the subject of this book. Dried poppy pods with stems can be purchased online. Typing "buy dried poppies" into any Internet search engine will bring up many sources. A couple of online sources for dried opium poppies are www.poppiesshop.com and www.cheappoppies.com. Most people who obtain poppies legally do so by purchasing the seeds and growing the flowers themselves. The poppy seeds available in bottles in most grocery stores' spice sections are of the same variety as the opium poppy *(Papaver somniferum)*.

Some of these seeds will grow if planted. However, most of them have been treated to make them nonviable. There are many sources online for purchasing viable poppy seeds. One can type "buy poppy seeds" or "buy papaver somniferum seeds" into any Internet search engine to find many sources for opium poppy seeds. There are many varieties of poppies, including *Papaver nudicaule* (Iceland poppy), *Papaver miyabeanum* (Pacino poppy), and *Papaver nudicale* (Matador poppy), but it is the *Papaver somniferum* (opium poppy) that produces opium. Here are some online sources for opium poppy seeds:

www.bouncingbearbotanicals.com
www.giftsfromtheancients.com
www.ethnobotanicals.com
www.poppiesshop.com

Growing Poppies

The opium poppy is an annual that grows to about three feet. The flowers come in a variety of colors, including white, purple, red, and pink. The petals of the flower are very thin and resemble crepe paper. Helpful information for growing poppies includes the following:

- Poppies can be grown in pots or in the ground. An all-purpose potting soil can be used to grow them, but they do best in a slightly acidic soil. They prefer a loose, slightly sandy soil, as opposed to a clay soil. Good drainage is also helpful.
- Plants should be spaced six to twelve inches apart. If planting a large area, a general rule is that one pound of poppy seeds should cover one acre. The seeds should be placed on the soil and a thin layer of soil should be placed over the top.
- If planting in the ground (as opposed to a pot), the ground should be tilled first. The soil should be kept moist, but not wet. Having the soil too wet can promote fungus and rotting. The young plants are delicate, so watering by misting or lightly sprinkling them is best. The plants typically take a week or two to sprout.

- Outside in areas where it freezes, the seeds should be planted after the last freeze. In areas without a freeze, they can be planted outside early to mid-March.
- A fertilizer appropriate for flowers should be used. Chicken manure, cow manure, or horse manure may also be used.
- Poppies require lots of sunlight. As the plant grows, the flower bud will appear. Some people recommend pulling off the first flower bud. They report that removing the first bud will cause the plant to grow several buds in its place.
- The plants should be watered until the petals grow from the flower bud. Watering should then be stopped. Some water may be given if the petals seem to wilt significantly. Watering the plant at this point may reduce the potency of the opium it produces.

After ten to fourteen days, the petals will fall off and the pod will begin to ripen. There are some differences of opinion as to when the poppy is then ready for the harvesting of opium, but ten days after the petals drop off seems to be a good estimate. In Hogshire's book (mentioned above), he says that the poppy bud will take on a "dusty or frosted" appearance when it is time to harvest the opium. At this point, the opium harvesting process can begin, or the poppies can be cut and dried to make opium tea.

Harvesting Opium

To extract the opium, the outermost part of the pod is scraped or cut. Cutting too deep, into where the seeds are, will result in some of the opium being lost inside of the seed pod. One must be delicate in this. Professional opium farmers have developed a variety of instruments for cutting the outside of the pod. Non-professionals typically use a pin, small needle, Exacto knife, razor, or very sharp knife. Once the outer layer of the pod is cut, opium beads will begin to seep out. Usually within a few hours, these beads of opium will turn to brown or black. They can then be scraped off using a dull knife or similar instrument.

Drying Opium Poppies

People dry poppies to save them for later use, to make opium tea, and also for making flower arrangements. After cutting, poppies can be dried by simply placing them somewhere warm and dry. They can also be placed in the sun to dry. Packing the poppies too close together will slow the drying process.

Making Opium Tea from Dried Poppies

The following information is based on contents from Jim Hogshire's book, *Opium for the Masses*. About ten dried poppy pods should make tea for one person.

Break off the stems from the base of the poppy pods. If done right, this will leave a hole in the bottom of the pod. Otherwise, make a small hole in the bottom of the pod. Shake the seeds out of the pod and put them aside. The seeds can be used to plant more poppies or can be used for poppy seed bread, and so forth. Break the pods up a little with your fingers while placing them into a coffee grinder, then grind. Boil about two cups of water. Remove the water and mix it very well with the ground poppy pods. Mixing can be done in a blender for a minute or two, with a hand mixer for a minute or two, or by stirring briskly with a spoon or whisk for a minute or two.

The mixture is then poured through a fine wire strainer. Some powder will pass through the strainer, but the strainer should be fine enough to catch most of the ground poppy. Using a spoon or your finger, press the rest of the water out of the ground poppy. The tea is then ready for drinking. The ground poppy left in the strainer can be used again, with about half as much water, to produce a second batch of poppy tea. The poppy stems can also be ground to make tea, but the tea will be less potent.

The opium tea can also be transferred into opium by evaporating the water. You cannot boil the tea to evaporate the water without losing opium. One method suggested by Hogshire is to place the tea in a cookie sheet or flat baking pan and put it in front of a fan. As the water evaporates, you can scrape up the opium left in the bottom of the pan. Of course, for this method the less dried poppy pod remains that get through your strainer, the better.

How People Use Opium to Get High

The smoking of opium is not done by burning it, as one would do with tobacco or marijuana. Opium is smoked by heating it indirectly. Typically a pea-size piece of opium is placed in a pipe or bong designed for opium smoking. Someone suggested that a freebase pipe would also work, but I do not have any information from anyone who has actually tried this method. Another method of smoking opium is to place it on a piece of tinfoil and heat it from below while sucking up the smoke from a straw. The only problem with this method is that some of the smoke is typically lost, though if no other method is available this does work.

Opium can also be taken orally. This is typically done by dissolving the opium in something like vodka first. A typical oral dosage is 50 to 200 milligrams. It is generally recommended to start with a low dose and work one's way up if needed to avoid the risk of overdose.

The Opium Experience

Effects of Opium

relief from pain

a feeling of relaxation and calm

decreased anxiety

slowed breathing and heart rate

impaired coordination

constricted pupils

nausea

constipation

The experience is almost always pleasurable, even euphoric. Smoking results in a rapid onset of pleasant relaxation. Oral ingestion of opium takes twenty to forty minutes for an effect. The effects last for one to three hours if smoked and two to six hours if taken orally.

Some Risks of Using Opium Poppies

The two largest risks of opium use are addiction and overdose. Opium can produce a psychological addiction as well as a physical addiction. Using opium frequently and long enough will result in physical addiction. Opium withdrawals are notoriously painful, but medical treatments can greatly reduce the pain of opium withdrawals.

It is recommended that if addiction to any of the opiates has occurred, you should check into a detox center to help with the withdrawal symptoms, and then enter into an addiction treatment program. Frequent, long-term opium use reduces the body's natural endorphin response. Thus, when one stops using opium, the brain lacks much of its natural mood elevator and pain reducer.

Opium overdose can also be a problem. This happens most often with taking opium orally (as opposed to smoking it). When one smokes opium, overdose is usually prevented because the effects are felt fairly rapidly and the individual will stop smoking once they are very high. In contrast, when taking opium orally, it takes some time for the effects to be felt. This delay makes it easy for someone to ingest an overdose of opium that does not hit them until later.

Side effects of opium use include itching and constipation. Pregnant and nursing women should not use opium. Opium addicts tend to not take very good care of themselves. Their self-neglect often results in malnutrition, weight loss, and overall poor physical health.

What Not to Do, Part 1
Inhaling Volatile Solvents and Aerosols (Huffing)

It may seem strange that a book that repeatedly reminds the reader that it is only for informational purposes and warns not to try any of the substances described has two appendices describing what substances to not do. I decided to place these substances, and the one described in the next appendix, in separate sections at the end of the book, because their dangers are so significant that the majority of the mind-altering substance literature and culture recommend against the use of these substances.

Any substance use, just like love and sex, has some risk associated with it. The substances described in this and the following appendix have such a higher likelihood of harm than those in the previous fourteen chapters, that to put them in the same place as the other substances in this book would be misleading to the reader.

Despite the grave danger of these substances, they are very commonly used as mind-altering agents. They can all be easily obtained legally. Even though there is a large amount of information in the literature about their dangerousness, their popularity continues.

Inhalants

Volatile solvents and aerosols are substances of this particularly dangerous type. They are part of a group of psychoactive substances called inhalants. This group of substances is usually divided into four categories:

1. Volatile solvents
2. Aerosols
3. Inhaled anesthetics
4. Inhaled nitrites

The inhaled anesthetics include nitrous oxide, which is the subject of a previous chapter and is of relatively low risk of harm. Additional inhaled anesthetics include ether, sevoflurane, desflurane, isoflurane, and halothane. None of these are commonly available. The inhaled nitrites are commonly referred to as "poppers."

The inhaled nitrites include amyl nitrite, butyl nitrite, and isobutyl nitrite. They were once popular legal recreational drugs in the United States. They are currently illegal to sell or distribute in the United States, but they are not illegal for an individual to possess. They continue to be legal in many other countries. Despite their being illegal to sell in the United States, several sites on the Internet located in foreign countries say they will send them to the United States. It may be that there would be no problem with buying inhaled nitrites from a foreign country for personal use.

The volatile solvents start to vaporize at room temperature. Some of the literature separates out fuels (e.g., gasoline) from the category of volatile solvents (e.g., paint thinner). However, these substances are used in mostly the same way and have similar effects, so here I will use the term volatile solvents to include fuels.

Volatile Solvents

acetone	kerosene
benzene	methanol
butane	methylene chloride
difluoroethane	naptha
ethanol	propane
ethyl acetate	toluene
gasoline	trichloromethane
hydrocarbons	xylene

These chemicals are found in some of the following products:

rubber cement, airplane glue, some model glues, nail polish remover, computer duster, paint thinner, spray paint, various cleaning fluids, spot remover, lighters, and some hair sprays.

Aerosols are particles of solids or liquids that are dispersed as a suspension in a gas. These are products contained in spray cans. Aerosols include fluorocarbons, which are contained in some air fresheners, hair sprays, and spray paints. Many spray paints also contain the volatile solvent toluene. Freon, which is used in air conditioners, is also a dangerous inhalant. Freon is being phased out, or already has been phased out, in many places due to its contributing to air pollution.

Huffing

The inhalation of volatile solvents and aerosols is commonly referred to as "huffing." Huffing can be done by placing the substance onto a towel or cloth and then placing it over the mouth or nose and breathing in through it. It is also done by inhaling the fumes of the substance directly from a container or by placing the substance in a paper or plastic bag and inhaling from it ("bagging"). Aerosols are sometimes sprayed directly into the nose or mouth. Some people even place the substance on their sleeve or other clothing so they can easily take their huffing with them.

Inhalation of these substances results in their being quickly absorbed from the lungs into the bloodstream. They quickly pass into the brain and other organs. The onset of effect is rapid from inhaling, and the high can last from a few minutes to over an hour. The effects of inhaling these substances can vary, but most commonly described effects are a feeling of drunkenness, euphoria, impaired coordination, and light-headedness. Some users report feeling stimulated, but most common are reports of feeling lethargic. Speech often is slurred, and the person usually appears to have been drinking alcohol.

Dangers of Inhaling Volatile Substances

liver damage	nerve damage
kidney damage	death
hearing loss	
limb spasms	*Note:* No other commonly used
convulsions	intoxicating substances cause as
brain damage	much damage to the body and brain.

The most common causes of death from huffing are due to the physical depressive effects and asphyxiation. The depressive effects of many of these substances can be so severe that breathing is impaired and even stops, resulting in death. The occurrence of life-threatening respiratory depression is more common than that from opiates like heroin or oxycodone. Asphyxiation from huffing is typically caused in one of two ways. The individual may throw up while passed out or sedated and choke on his own vomit. Depressed breathing can contribute to the likelihood of this occurring.

The other way for asphyxiation to occur is that the person simply does not breathe in enough oxygen. Placing a cloth or bag over the mouth and nose can interfere with the breathing of air. If the person becomes overly sedated or passes out and does not remove the cloth or bag from his face, death by asphyxiation can follow.

MRI scans of the brain show clear damage to the brains of chronic volatile substance users. Sudden sniffing death syndrome (SSDS) is the name given to a single session of volatile solvents/aerosol inhalant use that produces irregular heart rhythms, followed by heart failure and death. It can occur in a person who is in good health. The National Institute of Drug Abuse reports that 55 percent of deaths from volatile solvent/ aerosol inhalant use are due to SSDS. Of these deaths, 22 percent were reported to have occurred to individuals with no history of inhalant abuse.

Aside from the direct physical harm to the individual caused by huffing these psychoactive chemicals, there are indirect dangers as well. Many of the chemicals are flammable, and there are reports of individuals suffering burns while inhaling them too close to an open flame. These products also contain many chemicals besides the ones that cause the intoxication the user is seeking. Some of these chemicals can cause a wide variety of damages to the body. The impairing effects of inhaled substances have also resulted in serious accidents, including deaths due to driving under the influence. Inhaled volatile solvents and aerosols may also be harmful to a developing fetus, but the evidence is mixed in this area.

The use of volatile substances and aerosols is most often a young person's experiment. The age group with the highest use of these substances is eighth graders, though there are many cases of adults addicted to volatile solvents and aerosols. Its prevalence is probably due to these substances being so easily available to young people and the difficulty for young people to obtain other mind-altering substances, like alcohol and illegal drugs.

In conclusion, inhaling volatile solvents and aerosols is a common method of altering consciousness, especially among juveniles. To have excluded it from this book would have been to ignore the reality of legal substances people are using. Regardless, the majority opinion is that the risks and harm of inhaling volatile solvents and aerosols far outweigh the enjoyment or benefits.

What Not to Do, Part 2
Solanaceae Family of Plants
(Belladonna, Datura, Henbane, Mandrake)

Like the volatile solvents and inhalants described in the preceding appendix, the *Solanaceae* family of plants are commonly used for their psychoactive properties, but they have a significant risk of harm.

The *Solanaceae* family is a group of flowering plants often called the potato or nightshade family. Many of the plants in this family have been used by humans for hundreds, even thousands of years. The family includes the following:

datura (jimson weed, devil's apple, thorn apple, stink weed, moon flower)

belladonna (*Atropa belladonna*, deadly nightshade)

henbane (*Hyoscyamus niger*, stinking nightshade)

mandrake (*Mandragora officinarum*)

eggplant

potato

tobacco

tomato
petunia
chili peppers
paprika

The first four of these, datura, belladonna, henbane, and mandrake, have long been associated with witchcraft, and according to legend made up the witch's flying ointments. The ointments were supposedly rubbed on the body, allowing the witch to fly. The psychoactive effects of these plants may have contributed to the idea that they could make one fly. Many other members of the *Solanaceae* are used for food or their flowers are used for decorations.

The four legendary "witch plants" are the ones that have been used for their psychoactive properties and are therefore the ones that will be described here. In the United States, datura is the most commonly used of the four, with belladonna being the second most common. Henbane and mandrake are not often used in the United States, but there are a few reports regarding their use. All four are easily available on the Internet, making them more accessible than in the past. They may also be more commonly used in other countries.

There is one report from the 1980s of henbane use by children in Turkey. The children there used it as part of a game and for its intoxicating effects. Of the children described in the study, 26 percent of those who had used henbane needed to be hospitalized. Two of the children died as a result of their using it.

The identified psychoactive chemicals in these four members of the *Solanaceae* family are atropine, scopolamine,

hyoscine, and hyosciamine. These chemicals have anticho-
linergic properties, which is a primary mechanism of their
effect.

Effects of These Plants

---

delirium

stimulation

dilated pupils

nausea

rapid heartbeat

disorientation

changes in vision

sensitivity to light and sound

difficulty urinating

irritation of the mouth and throat

intense emotional experiences

Hallucinations are common in moderate to high doses.
These hallucinations are often described as different from
those induced by other substances, because it is common for
the individual to be unable to recognize that it is a hallucina-
tion and to differentiate it from reality. Blackouts or memory
loss are often reported after using these substances.

The majority of people who use these plants describe their
experience as negative. Most will not want to repeat the experience. Addiction to these plants is unlikely, because they
are not very enjoyable. Despite the negatives, some people will
still be repeat users of them.

It is unclear how many deaths each year are caused by these

plants, but there are many reports available on the Internet of deaths that have resulted from their use. The unpleasant effects experienced by most users of psychoactive *Solanaceae* plants, and the possibility of death, has led to the almost universal opinion that these plants are to be avoided.

Recommended Further Reading

Amaringo, P., & Luna, L. E. (1999). *Ayahuasca Visions,* North Atlantic Books.

Baker, P. (2003). *The Book of Absinthe: A Cultural History,* Grove Press.

Booth, M. (1999). *Opium: A History,* St. Martin's Press.

Cass, H., & McNally, T. (1998). *Kava: Nature's Answer to Stress, Anxiety, and Insomnia,* Prima Lifestyles.

Cheyene, S. (2006). *Salvia Divinorum,* Aardvark.

The Comprehensive Drug Abuse Prevention and Control Act of 1970 (1970).

Conner, K. M. (1999). *Kava: Nature's Stress Relief,* Avon Books.

Conrad, B. (1997). *Absinthe: History in a Bottle,* Chronicle Books.

D'Arcy, W. G. (1986). *Solanaceae Biology and Systematics,* Columbia University Press.

De Alverga, A. P. (1999). *Forest of Visions: Ayahuasca,*

Amazonian Spirituality, and the Santo Daime Tradition, Park Street Press.

The Declaration of Independence of the United States (1776).

De Quincey, Thomas (2003), original publication, 1821. *Confessions of an English Opium Eater,* Penguin Classics.

Eich, E. (2008). *Solanaceae and Convolvulaceae: Secondary Metabolites: Biosynthesis, Chemotaxonomy, Biological, and Economic Significance,* Springer.

Griffith, W. (1993). *Opium Poppy Garden: The Way of a Chinese Grower,* Ronin Publishing.

Gottlieb, A. (1997). *Peyote and Other Psychoactive Cacti,* Ronin Publishing.

Grauds, C. (1999). *The Natural Pharmacist: Your Complete Guide to Kava and Anxiety,* Prima Lifestyles.

Greenwood-Robinson, M. (1999). *Kava: Nature's Wonder Herb,* Dell.

Grof, S. (1994). *LSD Psychotherapy: Exploring the Frontiers of the Hidden Mind,* Hunter House.

Harris, B. (1976). *Growing Wild Mushrooms: A Complete Guide to Cultivating Edible and Hallucinogenic Mushrooms,* Wingbow Press.

Heinrich, C. (2002). *Magic Mushrooms in Religion and Alchemy,* Park Street Press.

Holtorf, K. (1998). *Urine Trouble,* Vandalay Press.

Hogshire, J. (1994). *Opium for the Masses: A Practical Guide to Growing Poppies and Making Opium,* Loompanics Unlimited.

Kilham, C. (2001). *Psyche Delicacies: Coffee, Chocolate, Chiles, Kava, and Cannabis, and Why They're Good for You,* Rodale.

Kilham, C. S. (1996). *Kava: Medicine Hunting in Paradise: The Pursuit of a Natural Alternative to Anti-Anxiety Drugs and Sleeping Pills,* Park Street Press.

Lebot, V., Merlin, M., & Lindstrom, L. (1997). *Kava: The Pacific Elixir: The Definitive Guide to Its Ethnobotany, History, and Chemistry,* Healing Arts Press.

Luna, E., & White, S. F. (2000). *Ayahuasca Reader: Encounters with the Amazon's Sacred Vine,* Synergetic Press.

Marnell, T. (2006). *Drug Identification Bible,* Amer-Chem.

Metzner, Ralph (2005). *Sacred Vine of Spirits: Ayahuasca,* Park Street Press.

———, Callaway, J. C., Grob, C. S., & McKenna, D. J. (1999). *Ayahuasca: Human Consciousness and the Spirits of Nature,* Thunder's Mouth Press.

Milton, G. (2000). *Nathaniel's Nutmeg: Or the True and Incredible Adventures of the Spice Trader Who Changed the Course of History,* Penguin.

Ott, J. (1996). *Pharmacotheon: Entheogenic Drugs, Their Plant Sources, and History,* Natural Products Co.

———. (1994). *Ayahuasca Analogs,* Jonathan Ott Books.

Peet, P. (Ed.) (2004). *Under the Influence: The Disinformation Guide to Drugs,* The Disinformation Company.

Reichert, R. (1997). *Kava Kava: The Anti-Anxiety Herb that Relaxes and Sharpens the Mind,* Keats Publishing.

Rudgley, R. (2000). *The Encyclopedia of Psychoactive Substances,* St. Martin's Press.

———. (1995). *Essential Substances: A Cultural History of Intoxicants in Society,* Kodansha Globe.

Sahelian, R. (1998). *Kava: The Miracle Antianxiety Herb,* St. Martin's Paperback.

Shanon, Benny (2003). *The Antipodes of the Mind: Charting the Phenomenology of the Ayahuasca Experience,* Oxford University Press: USA.

Shayan, S. (2001). *Divining Ecstasy: The Magical and Mystical Essence of Salvia Divinorun,* Loompanics Unlimited.

Sheldin, M., Wallechinsky, D., & Salver, S. (1993). *Laughing Gas: Nitrous Oxide,* Ronin Publishing.

Shulgin, A., & Shulgin, A. (1991). *PIHKAL: A Chemical Love Story,* Transform Press.

———. (1997). *TIHKAL: The Continuation,* Transform Press.

Siegel, R. K. (2005). *Intoxication: The Universal Drive for Mind-Altering Substances,* Park Street Press.

Singh, Y. N. (2004). *Kava: From Ethnology to Pharmacology,* CRC Press.

Sociedad Para La Preservation de Las Plartes del Mister, & Goire, R. G. (1998). *The Salvia Divinorum Grower's Guide,* Spectral Mindustries.

Stafford, P. (2005). *Heavenly Highs: Ayahuasca, Kava-Kava, DMT, and Other Plants of the Gods,* Ronin Publishing.

Torres, C. M., & Repke, D. B. (2006). *Anadenanthera: Visionary Plant of Ancient South America,* Haworth Press.

The United States Constitution (1791).

Walji, H. (1997). *Kava: Nature's Relaxant for Anxiety, Stress and Pain,* Hohm Press.

Wasson, R. G. (1968). *Soma: Divine Mushroom of Immortality,* Harcourt Brace Jovanovich.

Wilcox, Joan Parisi (2003). *Ayahuasca: The Visionary and Healing Powers of the Vine of the Soul,* Park Street Press.

World Health Organization (2004). *Betel-quid and Areca-nut Chewing and Some Areca-nut Derived Nitrosamines: Iarc Monographs (Iarc Monographs on the Evaluation of Carcinogenic Risks to Humans)*, World Health Organization.

Glossary

Agonist: a chemical that makes a nerve more likely to fire

Alkaloid: a large group of organic compounds that contain nitrogen

Antagonist: a chemical that makes a nerve less likely to fire

Ataxia: a failure of muscular coordination or irregularity of muscular action

Blood-brain barrier: term for a group of mechanisms associated with the brain vessel wall that control the movement of drugs and chemicals into the brain

Dissociative: a substance that produces a feeling of disconnection from oneself or one's senses

Hepatic system: related to the functions of the liver

Ketone: a substance produced by the body when blood sugar is low and fat is used by the body as fuel

Metabolite: a product produced by the body when it breaks down a substance, including waste products

Metabolize: the breaking down of substances by the cells of the body, such as occurs when the body converts food into energy

Mycorrhizal-symbiotic: the cooperative relationship between a fungus and the roots of a host tree

Neuron: nerve cell, basic cell of the nervous system

Neurotransmitter: chemical that allows communication between nerve cells

Overdose: taking too much of a substance or drug, resulting in illness, coma, or death

Psychedelic: a group of substances that have a common effect of altering one's perceptions/senses

Receptor: part of the nerve cell that allows chemicals to attach so that information can be communicated to the cell

Selective serotonin reuptake inhibitor (SSRI): chemical that causes serotonin to have a longer effect on a nerve cell, commonly used to treat depression and anxiety

Serotonin: neurotransmitter involved in mood, as well as many other functions

Spore: a reproductive cell for certain non-flowering plants, e.g., mushrooms

Synesthesia: blending of sensory experiences, e.g., seeing sounds

Tolerance: needing more of a substance to produce the same effects due to the body adjusting to repeated use of a substance

Withdrawal: symptoms experienced when a person physically addicted to a substance stops using the substance; they often appear as symptoms opposite the effect of the substance

Index